Acing

Administrative Law

A Checklist Approach to Solving Administrative Law Problems

Linda D. Jellum

Ellison Capers Palmer, Sr. Professor of Law
Mercer Law School

Series Editor

A. Benjamin Spencer

ACING SERIES®

WEST
ACADEMIC
PUBLISHING

Acing Series is a trademark registered in the U.S. Patent and Trademark Office.

© 2018 LEG, Inc. d/b/a West Academic
    444 Cedar Street, Suite 700
    St. Paul, MN 55101
    1-877-888-1330

West, West Academic Publishing, and West Academic are trademarks of West Publishing Corporation, used under license.

Printed in the United States of America

ISBN: 978-1-64020-695-3

To Kaylee, Chris, Susan, Lee, 4 ducks,
5 chickens, 4 cats, 1 dog, and Mr. Walt!

Preface

Administrative Law is a class about the procedures federal agencies must follow for their actions to be upheld if challenged. In short, agencies must jump through multiple hoops, and they must jump through those hoops properly. If you represent someone challenging an agency, your goal is either to make the agency start back at the beginning of the hoop-jumping process or to slow the hoop-jumping process down. Why? If you are lucky, a new administration (or president) who is more sympathetic to your client's point of view may come to office. If you represent an agency, your goal is to help it jump through the hoops properly so that if someone later challenges the agency, it is not told to start over. You might say that this book will help you learn how to hoop jump.

Why use this book to help you prepare for your exams in administrative law as opposed to all the other study aids that are available? When I was in law school, we used commercial outlines and hornbooks to help us study for exams. From those sources (and of course from our notes as well), we distilled hundreds of hours of classes and tremendous amounts of substantive material into digestible, short outlines. "Short" differed in length depending upon the author; however, each of us tried to draft an outline that would be useful to us as we took our exams, whatever "useful" meant. Longer outlines were more useful for open-book exams because they served as cheat sheets for when we forgot the exact wording; shorter outlines were more useful for closed-book exams because they helped us memorize the most important material.

While creating an outline may have helped us memorize the material and learn discrete topics within a particular subject, I am pretty sure that creating an outline did not help anyone learn the material as a coherent whole. What I mean is that outlining did not help us learn how the material we studied at the end of the semester related to the material we studied in the very first class.

The Acing Law series addresses this deficiency. The books in this series are designed to make you think about how a course works as a whole. You are directed to start at the beginning: What is the first question you should ask when faced with a family law, torts law, constitutional law, tax law, or administrative law issue? When you have answered that question, what do you ask next? And so on until you ask the last question you should ask. The books in this series are designed to help you approach your exams in an organized and logical manner, something outlines really do not do.

In closing, let me thank my research assistant, Jessica Lill, J.D. 2018, and my assistant, Cherie Jump. This book is publishable because of their help.

I would also like to thank Professor Nancy Levit for her support this year. Some masquerade. Nancy never does.

LINDA D. JELLUM

July 2018

Table of Contents

PREFACE V

Introduction 1

Chapter 1. Is There Agency Action? 3
Review 3
A.   What Is an Agency? 3
B.   What Type of Agency Action Is at Issue? 5
   1.   Agency Rulemaking & Adjudication 5
   2.   Agency Information Gathering 6
        Agency Action Checklist 7
        Illustrative Problems 9
        Problem 1.1 9
        Analysis 9
        Problem 1.2 9
        Analysis 9
        Points to Remember 10

Chapter 2. Does the Agency Have Authority to Act? 11
Review 11
A.   Non-Constitutional Constraints on an Agency's Power
     to Act 12
   1.   Congressional Constraints on an Agency's Power
        to Act 12
   2.   Executive Constraints on an Agency's Power to
        Act 13
B.   Constitutional Constraints on an Agency's Power to
     Act 14
   1.   Introduction to Formalism & Functionalism 14
        a.   Formalism 14
        b.   Functionalism 16
   2.   Delegating Legislative & Judicial Power 20
        a.   Delegating Legislative Power 20
        b.   Delegating Judicial Power 23
C.   Constitutional Constraints on Appointment &
     Removal 24
   1.   Overview 24
   2.   Appointment 25
   3.   Removal 26

Authority to Act Checklist.. 28
Illustrative Problems... 31
Problem 2.1 31
Analysis 31
Problem 2.2 31
Analysis 32
Points to Remember 32

Chapter 3. What Procedures Are Required for
Rulemaking?... **35**
Review 35
A.   Initiating a Rulemaking.. 35
B.   Types of Rules & Rulemaking Procedures.................... 36
      1.   Types of Rules 37
      2.   Types of Rulemaking 37
            a.   Formal Rulemaking 37
            b.   Notice & Comment Rulemaking Procedures............ 38
            c.   Publication Procedures................................. 40
            d.   Hybrid Procedures 40
      3.   Summary of Types of Rules & Rulemaking 41
C.   Choosing the Appropriate Rulemaking Procedure.................. 41
      1.   Formal Rulemaking v. Notice & Comment
            Rulemaking 41
      2.   Notice & Comment Rulemaking v. Publication
            Rulemaking 42
            Procedures Required for Rulemaking: Checklist.............. 44
            Illustrative Problems...................................... 50
            Problem 3.1 50
            Analysis 50
            Problem 3.2 50
            Analysis 51
            Points to Remember 51

Chapter 4. What Procedures Are Required for
Adjudication? **53**
Review 53
A.   Orders and Adjudications 53
      1.   Choosing the Appropriate Adjudication Procedure.......... 53
B.   Formal Adjudication and Rulemaking Procedures 54
      1.   Notice.. 54
      2.   The Hearing 55
      3.   The Presiding Officer.. 55
      4.   Separation of Functions 56
      5.   Ex Parte Communications 57
      6.   The Initial Decision 58

        7. Appealing the Initial Decision to the Agency 59
    C. Informal Adjudication Procedures... 60
        1. APA Procedures 60
        2. Due Process Procedures 60
            Procedures Required for Adjudication: Checklist........... 61
            Illustrative Problems... 67
            Problem 4.1 67
            Analysis 67
            Problem 4.2 68
            Analysis 68
            Points to Remember 70

**Chapter 5. What Procedures Are Required for
    Investigation & Disclosure?** **71**
Review... 71
A. Agency Power to Investigate... 71
    1. Documents and Testimony... 72
        a. Voluntary Production 72
        b. Involuntary Production 72
    2. Inspections 73
        a. Voluntary Compliance.. 73
        b. Involuntary Compliance... 74
B. Agency Duty to Disclose... 75
    1. The Freedom of Information Act.. 75
    2. The Government in Sunshine Act 77
    3. The Federal Advisory Committee Act 79
        Procedures Required for Investigation: Checklist........... 80
        Illustrative Problems... 84
        Problem 5.1 84
        Analysis 85
        Problem 5.2 85
        Analysis 85
        Points to Remember 86

**Chapter 6. Is Judicial Review of the Agency's Action
    Available?**.. **89**
Review... 89
A. The Court & the Claim... 90
    1. Jurisdiction 90
    2. Cause of Action 90
        a. Agency Action.. 91
        b. Statutory Preclusion.. 91
        c. Committed to Agency Discretion 93
B. The Plaintiff... 93
    1. Constitutional Standing Requirements 93

           a.   Injury in Fact 94

           b.   Causation.. 94

           c.   Redressability... 95

     2.   Prudential Standing Requirements................................ 95

     3.   Statutory Standing Requirements: Zone of
         Interests 97

     4.   Standing Requirements: Summary 97

C.   The Timing... 98

     1.   Finality.. 98

     2.   Exhaustion 99

     3.   Ripeness 100

     4.   Timing Requirements: Summary 101

         Availability Checklist.. 102

         Illustrative Problems.. 109

         Problem 6.1 109

         Analysis... 109

         Problem 6.2 110

         Analysis... 110

         Points to Remember 112

Chapter 7. What Standard of Review Applies?...................... 113

Review 113

A.   Defining Questions of Fact & Policy.................................... 114

     1.   Questions of Fact 114

     2.   Questions of Policy & Discretion 115

B.   Standards of Review for Questions of Fact & Policy............. 115

     1.   Substantial Evidence... 115

     2.   Arbitrary & Capricious.. 116

     3.   Arbitrary & Capricious Review v. Substantial
         Evidence Review 118

C.   Defining Questions of Law & Mixed Questions...................... 119

     1.   Questions of Law 119

     2.   Mixed Questions/Questions of Law Application 119

D.   Standards of Review for Mixed Questions & Pure
   Questions of Law 120

     1.   Mixed Questions of Law & Fact................................... 120

     2.   Questions of Law 120

         a.   Agency Interpretation of Statutes 120

             i.   Skidmore.. 121

             ii.   Chevron.. 121

             iii.   Brand X.. 123

b. Agency Interpretations of Regulations 123
Standard Checklist 124
Illustrative Problems 128
Problem 7.1 128
Analysis 129
Problem 7.2 130
Analysis 131
Points to Remember 132

Chapter 8. The Big Picture **135**
The Entire Checklist 135
Illustrative Problems 167
Long Essay Problem 8-1 167
Analysis 172

Acing
Administrative Law

A Checklist Approach to Solving
Administrative Law Problems

Introduction

This book, Acing Administrative Law, will prepare you to take exams in Administrative Law (or even Leg/Reg). I have focused on the seven topics that you will most likely encounter on an essay exam. Because I could not cover every possible topic, I have chosen to focus on the topics on which you are most likely to be tested.

I have started differently than your law school course likely started. The first question I recommend you ask before every Administrative Law based exam question is: "What kind of agency action is at issue?" That question is important because the proper analysis of any administrative law issue flows from the type of action at issue. For example, if the agency engaged in rulemaking, you should ask whether the delegated authority violates the non-delegation doctrine; whether formal rulemaking procedures were necessary; whether notice-and-comment procedures were required or could be avoided; whether appropriate rulemaking procedures were followed; whether, during the rulemaking process, the agency decided a question of policy, fact, or law; and whether judicial review is available.

If instead the agency engaged in adjudication, then you should see if the delegated authority violates the very confusing public-private rights distinction; whether formal or informal adjudication was required; whether appropriate adjudication procedures were followed; whether, during the adjudication, the agency decided a question of fact, policy, or law; and whether judicial review is available.

Once you know the answers to these questions, you will need to determine whether the appropriate standard of judicial review for the agency's findings is substantial evidence, arbitrary and capricious review, *Chevron* analysis, *Skidmore* analysis, or *Auer* analysis. Just to warn you, you will be asked a standard of review question. I guarantee that!

Each chapter follows the series format. First, there is a brief (very brief) overview of the law in the area; followed by a chapter checklist; followed by two hypothetical problems, which are resolved using the chapter's checklist. Finally, each chapter concludes with a "Points to Remember" section to help remind you of the most important points in that chapter. However, this book differs from others in the series in that the final chapter is a master checklist followed by a comprehensive exam question, which is resolved using the master checklist. This unique feature of this Acing Book accomplishes exactly what I identified above: a way of understanding the course as a coherent whole.

As I conclude, let me caution that this book is not a substitute for thoroughly understanding the material. Rather, it is meant to help you organize the complex and overwhelming material you will need to learn in a way that may prove useful to you as you attempt to answer an exam question in this area. Most importantly, your professor may have a unique focus or understanding of administrative law, particularly those areas that are unsettled. When there is conflict between us: your professor wins.

CHAPTER 1

Is There Agency Action?

A gencies regulate private conduct, administer entitlement programs, collect taxes, deport aliens, issue permits, run the space program, manage the national parks, and so on. Simply put, agencies run the functions we think of as government, whether state or federal. Of more interest to us is how agencies do what they do, which the Administrative Procedures Act (APA)[1] governs.

The APA identifies an agency's procedural law, which we call *administrative law*. Pursuant to the APA and other laws, agencies must follow particular procedures to act legally. In essence, agencies must jump through the appropriate hoops. If the agency misses a hoop, jumps through the wrong hoop, or fails to jump at all, the agency has not followed proper procedures and must generally begin its process again. Hence, here are the first of two questions you must ask yourself as you approach an administrative law exam: (1) whether the actor is an *agency*, and (2) whether the agency acted via rulemaking, adjudication, or inspection/investigation. In other words, has an *agency* issued a *rule* through rulemaking, an *order* through adjudication, or a subpoena or request for information?

REVIEW

A. What Is an Agency?

First, you must first confirm that it was indeed an *agency* that acted. The APA broadly defines "agency" as "each authority of the Government of the United States . . . not includ[ing Congress, the courts, state governments, etc.]."[2] Thus, the term "agency" includes all governmental authorities including administrations (*e.g.*, the Small Business Administration), commissions (*e.g.*, the Commodity

---

[1]   5 U.S.C. § 551 *et. seq.* (2012) (hereinafter "APA").
[2]   APA §§ 551(1) & 701 (2012).

Futures Trading Commission), corporations (*e.g.*, the Federal Deposit Insurance Corporation), boards (National Transportation Safety Board), departments (*e.g.*, the U.S. Department of Education), divisions (*e.g.*, the NWRS Division of Refuge Law Enforcement), and agencies (e.g., the Defense Health Agency). While the definition is broad, the president is not an agency.[3]

There are two types of agencies: independent agencies and executive agencies. Independent agencies are believed to be less subject to the president's influence because they are usually headed by multimember groups[4] from both political parties, who serve specific terms and can typically only be removed for cause. Examples of independent agencies include the Securities and Exchange Commission, the Federal Trade Commission, the Federal Election Commission, the Equal Opportunity Commission, and the National Labor Relations Board.

In contrast, executive agencies are headed by individuals (generally called secretaries), who the president appoints, with the advice and consent of the Senate, and who serve at the discretion of the president. Examples include the Department of Defense, the Homeland Security Administration, and the Department of Education. The largest and most influential executive agencies are called departments; departments contain a host of sub-agencies. The heads of the departments are known collectively as the cabinet. Agencies must follow the same procedures when they promulgate a rule or when they issue an order regardless of whether they are independent or executive. Thus, the type of agency is irrelevant for purposes of this chapter; however, you may have to address the constitutionality of an independent agency's structure, including appointment and removal. We will address this issue further in Chapter 2.

After determining that the actor is an agency, you should ensure that the agency acted in some way. Often, agency action is easy to identify: a rule is promulgated, an order is entered, or an inspection takes place. But sometimes action is more difficult to identify. For example, an agency might unreasonably delay acting or fail to act at all when legally required to act. Both of these behaviors are defined as "actions" under the APA. The APA defines *agency action* to include "the failure to act"[5] when action is

---

[3]   Franklin v. Massachusetts, 505 U.S. 788, 796 (1992).

[4]   There are a few exceptions; for example, a single individual heads the Consumer Financial Protection Bureau, yet it is an independent agency. A divided D.C. Court of Appeals held that this structure does not violate the Appointments Clause of the U.S. Constitution. PHH Corp. v. CFPB, 881 F.3d 75, 110 (D.C. Cir. 2018).

[5]   APA § 551(13) (2012).

required.[6] Also, a court can "compel agency action unlawfully withheld or unreasonably delayed."[7]

Assuming the agency acted, failed to act, or unreasonably delayed acting, your next step is to determine what kind of action is at issue. Agencies act in three ways: by rulemaking, by adjudicating, and by gathering and disseminating information. Agencies act like legislatures when they make rules through rulemaking, like courts when they issue orders through adjudication, and like the police when they gather information through investigation. Depending on the type of action, different procedural requirements apply.

B.   What Type of Agency Action Is at Issue?

The APA requires agencies to use different procedures for rulemaking, adjudication, and information gathering. Hence, correctly classifying any given agency action is essential. Usually, you will have little difficulty identifying the correct category; however, sometimes this determination will be more difficult. When in doubt, you should begin with the idea that if the action is more like what a legislature does, then the action is likely rulemaking culminating in a rule. Instead, if the action is more like what a court does, then the action is likely an adjudication culminating in an order. To confirm your gut reaction, apply the APA's definitions of "rule" and "order," which are arguably somewhat circular.

1.   Agency Rulemaking & Adjudication

Typically if you have difficulty identifying agency action, the choice is either rulemaking or adjudication. The APA defines "adjudication" as the "agency process for the formulation of an order."[8] An "order" is defined as "the whole or part of a final disposition . . . of an agency in a matter other than *rulemaking*, but including licensing."[9] "Rulemaking" is defined as the "agency process for formulating, amending, or repealing a *rule*."[10] A "rule" is defined as "an agency statement of general . . . applicability and future effect designed to implement, interpret, or prescribe law or

---

[6]   See, e.g., Massachusetts v. EPA, 549 U.S. 497, 517 (2007).

[7]   APA § 706(1) (2012). Typically, unreasonable-delay challenges relate to an agency's failure to act on a rulemaking petition as APA § 553(e) requires. To determine whether the agency's delay was reasonable, a reviewing court will apply the TRAC's factors. Telecommunications Research & Action Ctr. v. FCC, 750 F.2d 70, 76 (identifying the following factors: whether the applicable statute contains a timetable, whether delay would impact human welfare, how forcing a decision would affect higher agency priorities, and how all the interests would be affected).

[8]   APA § 551(7) (2012).

[9]   APA § 551(6) (2012).

[10]   APA § 551(5) (2012).

policy."[11] Pursuant to these definitions, rules, like statutes, are general laws that apply prospectively to multiple people and entities, while adjudications are specific laws that apply retroactively to the parties. Years ago, I had a student submit a drawing to depict the difference between an order and a rule. For rulemaking, the student drew a bus heading down the freeway with all the passengers looking forward. For adjudication, the student drew a Volkswagen bug, stopped on the road with its driver looking backward.

Let's be clear about one thing, agencies may choose to regulate using either procedure. So long as an agency has authority to act using either process (check the enabling statute), the decision whether to proceed through rulemaking or adjudication is vested, primarily, in the informed discretion of the agency. In *Chenery II*, the Supreme Court recognized that, although an agency should consider making policy as much as possible using rulemaking, agencies must have flexibility to deal with regulatory problems in the manner they deem most appropriate.[12]

Although the decision whether to proceed through rulemaking or adjudication is primarily vested in the informed discretion of the agency, courts may set aside an agency's order if the agency's decision to use adjudication amounts to an abuse of discretion. For example, were an agency to impose a substantial penalty or liability on a regulated person or entity for violating a legal principle that had not been previously announced, the agency's order may be set aside.[13]

2. Agency Information Gathering

The last possible type of agency action that may be at issue we will call "informational." Informational actions include investigative actions like an inspection, a request to an entity to voluntarily provide information, and a demand to an entity to produce information (a subpoena). They also include disclosures, like providing information to the public, holding open meetings, and allowing access to certain information.

---

[11] APA § 551(4) (2012).

[12] SEC v. Chenery Corp., 332 U.S. 194, 202–03 (1947) (saying that an agency "may not have had sufficient experience with a particular problem to warrant rigidifying its tentative judgment into a hard and fast rule. Or the problem may be so specialized and varying in nature as to be impossible of capture within the boundaries of a general rule.").

[13] *See, e.g.*, NLRB v. Bell Aerospace Co. Div. of Textron Inc., 416 U.S. 267, 295 (1974). A regulated person's or entity's substantial reliance on the agency's prior practice may, in some cases, also warrant the setting aside of an agency order.

To effectively regulate, agencies need information and lots of it. To believe that its government is acting legitimately, the public demands transparency. Hence, information flows in both directions: from the public to the agency and from the agency to the public.

Unlike rulemaking and adjudication, the APA does not address an agency's ability to seek information from those it regulates, known as regulated entities.[14] Rather, the agency's enabling statute and the Constitution regulate this area.[15] Similarly, the APA does not address an agency's duty to provide information to the public. Rather, other statutes do so, such as the Freedom of Information Act,[16] the Government in Sunshine Act,[17] the Federal Advisory Act,[18] the Privacy Act,[19] among others. If your issue relates to an informational action, then you need to determine whether the agency is seeking information from a regulated entity or someone is seeking information from the agency.

After you have identified that *an agency* has acted or failed to act and the type of agency action, you can proceed to the steps in the next chapter.

AGENCY ACTION CHECKLIST

A. *Agency* Action—Is the actor an authority of the United States government, such as an administration, commission, corporation, board, department, division, or agency?

  1. **No**—If no, the actor is not an agency, and the APA does not apply. The president, Congress, a federal court, a state or territorial government, a military commission or court martial, and specifically exempted authorities under APA §§ 551(1)(A)–(H) are not agencies. Stop here.

  2. **Yes**—If yes, the actor is a federal agency, and administrative law applies. Proceed to B. below.

B. **Agency** *Action*—Did the agency act, fail to act, or unreasonably delay acting?

---

[14] Regulated entities can be individuals or businesses.
[15] Specifically, the Fourth and Fifth Amendments apply.
[16] APA § 552 (Supp. 2016).
[17] *Id.*
[18] 5 U.S.C. App. 2.
[19] APA § 552a (Supp. 2016).

1. **No**—If the agency did not act and was not required to act or if the agency did not unreasonably delay acting, then the APA does not apply. <u>Stop here.</u>

2. **Yes**—If the agency acted or failed to act when legally required, the APA applies. <u>Proceed to C. below.</u> If the agency unreasonably delayed acting, then the APA applies. To determine whether the agency's delay was reasonable, a reviewing court will apply the TRAC factors. *Telecommunications Research & Action Ctr v. FCC*, 750 F.2d 70, 76 (D.C. Cir. 1984) (identifying the following factors: whether the applicable statute contains a timetable, whether delay will impact human welfare, how forcing a decision would affect higher agency priorities, and how all the interests are affected). <u>Proceed to C. below.</u>

C. **Agency *Action***—How did the agency act?

1. **Rulemaking**—Did the agency promulgate a general rule with future application?

   a. **No**—If no, the agency may have acted using adjudicatory powers. <u>Proceed to C.2. below.</u>

   b. **Yes**—If yes, the agency acted via rulemaking, and the APA applies. <u>Proceed to Chapter 2.</u>

2. **Adjudication**—Did the agency issue an order that applies to specific parties and their past actions?

   a. **No**—If no, the agency may have acted using informational powers. <u>Proceed to C.3. below.</u>

   b. **Yes**—If yes, the agency acted using adjudication, and the APA applies. Ask whether the agency legitimately choose to use adjudication rather than rulemaking to make a new policy?

      i. **No**—If a party was substantially penalized for abiding by prior policy, then the agency's choice is invalid, and any order should be set aside. *NLRB v. Bell Aerospace Co. Div. of Textron Inc.*, 416 U.S. 267 (1974). <u>Stop here.</u>

      ii. **Yes**—If yes, the agency's choice is valid. <u>Proceed to Chapter 2.</u>

3. **Information Gathering**—Did the agency seek information through an inspection, with a request for information, or by subpoena?

a. **No**—If no, you have reached a wrong answer at some point in your analysis. <u>Start over</u>.

b. **Yes**—If yes, the agency acted using executive powers and administrative law applies, but not the APA. <u>Proceed to Chapter 2</u>.

ILLUSTRATIVE PROBLEMS

■ PROBLEM 1.1 ■

Assume that the Federal Housing Authority (FHA) decides to stop insuring Capital Mortgage, Inc.'s single-family home mortgages because of alleged irregularities in its accounting practices. You work for Capital Mortgage. What questions should you ask in evaluating how to proceed?

Analysis

This issue here is whether an agency acted and whether that action was rulemaking or adjudication. Using the checklist above (A & C), you should ask first whether the FHA is an authority of the United States government. APA § 551(1). It is.

You should determine next how the agency acted. Here the rule does have prospective effect; however, the rule applies only to one company and is based on that company's prior actions. Hence, the FHA issued an order and must follow the requirements in the APA and the Constitution's Due Process clause when it acts. Finally, the agency's decision to act using adjudication in this case would be valid. If Capital Mortgage were substantially penalized for abiding by prior policy, then the agency's choice would be invalid, and any order should be set aside. *NLRB v. Bell Aerospace Co. Div. of Textron Inc.*, 416 U.S. 267 (1974).

■ PROBLEM 1.2 ■

Assume that the automobile industry petitions the Department of Transportation (DOT) to modify a rule pertaining to use of airbags in compact vehicles and that the industry files a formal, written petition requesting the rule modification. You work as general counsel for DOT, which does not want to act on the petition at all or wants to delay immediate action. How would you advise DOT to respond to the petition, if at all?

Analysis

This issue here is whether the agency can ignore the petition or delay responding. After confirming the DOT is an agency (using checklist A above), use the checklist (B) above to ask next whether the agency is required to act. The APA does direct agencies to respond to petitions for rulemaking. Thus, the agency is required to act. However, the APA does not set forth how quickly an agency must act on a petition. A reviewing court will apply the TRAC factors to determine whether the agency's delay is unreasonable. *Telecommunications Research & Action Ctr. v. FCC*, 750 F.2d 70, 76 (D.C. Cir. 1984). Those factors include the following: (1) whether the applicable statute contains a timetable, (2) whether delay will impact human welfare, (3) how forcing a decision would affect higher agency priorities, and (4) how all the interests are affected. Thus, you should check the relevant enabling statute to see if Congress provided a timetable (usually not), explain why delay will not negatively impact human health (which may be difficult for airbag safety), detail the other agency priorities (perhaps explain other rulemakings the agency is involved in), and downplay the impact on the automobile industry and general public.

POINTS TO REMEMBER

- Administrative law, and specifically the APA, governs the procedures agencies must use when they promulgate rules via rulemaking or orders via adjudication. If an agency is not the actor, administrative law is not relevant.

- Agencies act like legislatures when they promulgate general rules with future applicability. They act like courts when the issue orders that apply to specific parties based on their past conduct. They act like police when they investigate and seek information.

- So long as Congress authorizes agencies to act either through rulemaking or adjudication, agencies have the discretion to choose to create policy using either procedure.

- The procedures an agency must follow according to the APA depend on whether the agency is promulgating a rule or issuing an order. Therefore, determining what action the agency is taking is the first step in determine what procedures the agency must follow.

- Agencies may not fail to act when required nor unreasonably delay acting.

CHAPTER 2

Does the Agency Have Authority to Act?

A fter determining the type of action, the next step is to determine whether the specific agency had authority to act in the way it did. To answer this question, we will look at whether the agency had statutory and constitutional power to act. And we will look at limits on that power. Additionally, we will look at a second issue related to constitutional authority: the appointment and removal of agency personnel

REVIEW

Agencies have no inherent power. For an agency to have power to act, Congress must first enact a statute that both creates the agency (if it does not already exist) and identifies the agency's powers and regulatory agenda. This authorizing statute is known as the *enabling*, or organic, statute. You should check to be sure that Congress has actually delegated authority to the agency to act as it did; in other words, did Congress give the agency authority to conduct rulemakings, adjudications, and inspections? If the enabling statute does not include such authority, another statute might. For example, the Environmental Protection Agency (EPA) was established through Reorganization Plan No. 3, an executive order President Richard Nixon issued, which Congress later enacted into law. Thus, this act created the EPA; however, other acts authorize the EPA to regulate specific topics. For example, the Clean Air Act, Clean Water Act, and the Toxic Substances Control Act all authorize the EPA to engage in rulemaking to increase the safety of air, water, and toxic substances. In addition, some acts and executive orders limit an agency's exercise of authority. We will explore some of these limiting laws below.

Lastly, and most importantly, the Constitution and its principle of separation of powers places limits on Congress's ability to delegate legislative and judicial powers. The Constitution places limits both on what can be delegated and to whom Congress can delegate. The latter limits are found in the appointment clause. Hence, after you have determined that an agency acted using either rulemaking or adjudication, you must next determine whether Congress legitimately delegated that specific power to that agency and whether the officials from that agency were constitutionally appointed.

A. Non-Constitutional Constraints on an Agency's Power to Act

1. Congressional Constraints on an Agency's Power to Act

While Congress can limit any type of agency activity, Congress typically focuses on retaining control over agency rulemaking. For example, in 1996, Congress enacted the Congressional Review Act, under which agencies must send all new rules to the Comptroller General.[1] Major rules are stayed for sixty days. A major rule is one whose annual economic impact is greater than $100 million. If desired, Congress can use a fast-track process to pass a joint resolution disapproving the rule, which must be signed by the president. Until 2017, Congress had "vetoed" only one agency regulation (a 2001 Clinton-era OSHA ergonomics regulation); however, since the 2016 election in which Republicans took control of Congress and the White House, Congress has used this procedure to roll back fourteen Obama-era regulations.

Other statutes with procedural requirements include the Regulatory Flexibility Act, which requires agencies to create a Regulatory Flexibility Analysis for any proposed rule that will significantly impact a substantial number of small businesses, organizations, or governments.[2] Also, the Unfunded Mandates Reform Act requires agencies to prepare a statement assessing the effect of any proposed regulation that will cause state, local, or tribal governments to incur more than $100 million annually.[3]

Sometimes, the Supreme Court strikes down these creative control attempts as unconstitutional. For example, the Court struck down legislative veto provisions in *INS v. Chadha*.[4] The legislative veto allowed Congress to delegate lawmaking authority to the

---

[1]   5 U.S.C. §§ 801–08 (2012).

[2]   5 U.S.C. § 601 *et seq.* (2012).

[3]   2 U.S.C. § 1501 *et seq.* (2012).

[4]   462 U.S. 919, 954–55 (1983).

executive, but reserved, either to a single chamber of Congress or to a committee from a single chamber, the power to oversee and veto the executive's use of this delegated authority.[5] Because legislative veto provisions allowed one chamber of Congress to unilaterally amend legislation and thereby avoid constitutionally required bicameral passage and presentment, the Court held that these provisions were unconstitutional.[6]

While it is unlikely that you will be expected to memorize the particulars of any of these statutes, you will be expected to be aware that statutes other than the enabling statute exist and place additional procedural requirements on agencies, typically when they wish to promulgate a rule.

2. Executive Constraints on an Agency's Power to Act

In addition to the statutes identified above, another limiting source you should consider is executive orders (E.O.). Presidents issue executive orders to tell agencies how to implement laws during that administration.

The most well-known executive order is E.O. 12,866. This executive order was initially issued by President Reagan, who campaigned on a platform of deregulation in the 1980s. E.O. 12,291 (its original number),[7] directed all executive agencies to perform a regulatory analysis assessing the costs and benefits of any "major" proposed regulations.[8] One of Reagan's purposes for issuing this executive order was to limit unnecessary regulation. However, each president since Reagan has reissued this order, albeit with slight changes. Today, it is known as E.O. 12,866.

Executive Order 12,866 provides that agencies may promulgate regulations only when they are "required by law," "necessary to interpret the law," or "are made necessary by compelling public need," such as material failures of private markets to protect or improve the health and safety of the public, the environment, or the well-being of the American people."[9] Agencies must follow specific procedural steps when developing regulatory priorities.[10]

---

[5]   462 U.S. at 954.

[6]   462 U.S. at 954–55.

[7]   E.O. 12,866 § 1, 58 Fed. Reg. 51735 (October 4, 1993).

[8]   E.O. 12,291, 3 C.F.R. § 127 (1982).

[9]   E.O. 12,866 § 1(a), 58 Fed. Reg. 51735 (October 4, 1993).

[10]   These procedures include (1) identifying the problem the regulation was intended to address, including "the failures of private markets or public institutions that warrant new agency action;" (2) determining whether the problem could be addressed through modifications to existing regulations or laws; (3) assessing alternatives to regulation, such as economic incentives; (4) considering "the degree and nature of the risks posed by various substances or activities" within the agency's

Specifically, when deciding whether a regulation is necessary, agencies must assess the costs and benefits of the regulatory alternatives, "including the alternative of not regulating."[11] The Office of Information and Regulatory Affairs (OIRA), which is located within the Office of Management and Budget (OMB), will review the proposed rule and analysis to ensure compliance with E.O. 12,866.

B.   Constitutional Constraints on an Agency's Power to Act

1.   *Introduction to Formalism & Functionalism*

In determine the legitimacy of constitutional constraints, you may be expected to know the difference between formalism and functionalism. The Supreme Court has approached questions involving separation of powers issues in two different ways, one of which is more accepting of overlap, the other which is not. Legal scholars have identified these two approaches as *formalism* and *functionalism*.

a.   Formalism

The *formalist* approach to separation of powers emphasizes the necessity of maintaining three distinct branches of government, each with delegated powers: one branch legislates, one branch executes, and one branch adjudicates. These powers come from the vesting clauses of the U.S. Constitution. Article I vests in Congress "[a]ll legislative Powers herein granted."[12] Legislative power is the power "to promulgate generalized standards and requirements of citizen behavior or to dispense benefits—to achieve, maintain, or avoid particular social policy results."[13] Congress alters legal rights through enacting, amending, and repealing statutes.

---

jurisdiction; (5) fashioning regulations "in the most cost-effective manner;" (6) assessing the costs and benefits, such that benefits justify the costs; (7) basing decisions "on the best reasonably obtainable scientific, technical, economic, and other information;" (8) recommending performance-based solutions rather than behavioral ones, when possible; (9) consulting with state, local, and tribal governments and assessing the impacts of regulations on these local governments; (10) avoiding duplications and inconsistencies among federal agencies; (11) minimizing the burdens; (12) considering the cumulative costs of regulation; and (13) writing all regulations in language that the general public can easily understand. E.O. 12,866 §§ 1(b)(1)–(12), 58 Fed. Reg. 51735 (October 4, 1993).

[11]   E.O. 12,866 § 1(a), 58 Fed. Reg. 51735 (October 4, 1993).

[12]   U.S. CONST. art. 1, § 1.

[13]   Martin H. Redish & Elizabeth J. Cisar, *"If Angels Were to Govern": The Need for Pragmatic Formalism in Separation of Powers Theory*, 41 DUKE L.J. 449, 479 (1991); *accord* INS v. Chadha, 462 U.S. 919, 952 (1983).

Article II of the Constitution vests "[t]he executive Power . . . in a President of the United States of America."[14] Executive acts are those in which an executive official exercises judgment about how to apply law to a given situation.[15] For the executive to execute the law there must be existing law to execute. In other words, while the legislature enacts laws, the executive enforces those laws.

Article III of the Constitution vests "[t]he judicial Power of the United States, . . . in one supreme Court, and in such inferior Courts as the Congress may from time to time ordain and establish."[16] Judicial power is the power to interpret laws and resolve legal disputes. "[T]o declare what the law is, or has been, is a judicial power, to declare what the law shall be is legislative."[17] The judiciary interprets laws by adjudicating cases and rendering dispositive judgments based on findings of law and fact; indeed, this is a court's primary power.

When confronting an issue raising separation of powers concerns, a formalist uses a two-step, rule-based approach. First, the formalist will identify the power being exercised: legislative, judicial, or executive. Second, the formalist will determine whether the appropriate branch is exercising that power in accordance with the Constitution. A formalist will, therefore, categorize the activity as legislative, executive, or judicial, and then analyze whether the appropriate branch is performing the activity. The chart below illustrates formalism in a very simplified way.

---

[14]   U.S. CONST. art. II, § 1, cl. 1.

[15]   Bowsher v. Synar, 478 U.S. 714, 732–33 (1986).

[16]   U.S. CONST. art. III, § 1.

[17]   Koshkonong v. Burton, 104 U.S. 668, 678 (1881) (*quoting* Ogden v. Blackledge, 6 U.S. 272, 277 (1804)).

FORMALISM

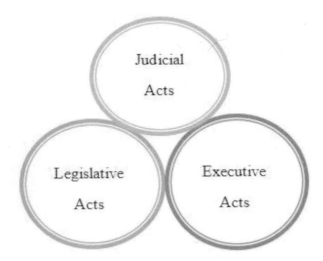

Each branch may constitutionally perform any function that falls within its corresponding "Acts Circle," but may not constitutionally perform any function that falls within another branch's "Acts Circle." Under formalism, a branch violates separation of powers when it attempts to exercise a power that is not constitutionally delegated to it (or not within its Acts Circle). Overlap is permitted only when constitutionally prescribed. So, for example, the president and Senate both play a role in appointing principal officers without violating separation of powers, because the Constitution delegates this power to both the executive and legislative branches.[18]

      b.   Functionalism

Functionalism's focus differs from formalism's focus. While formalists focus on strict separation, functionalists focus on balancing the inevitable overlap of powers to preserve the core functions the Constitution assigns to each branch. To maintain a relatively balanced power distribution, functionalists believe that a complete bar against any encroachment between the branches is unnecessary. Instead, functionalists focus on limiting encroachments into the core, constitutionally-appointed functions of each branch.

---

[18]   U.S. CONST. art. II § 2 cl. 2.

For example, the executive's power of appointment is a core function.[19] However, the appointment power is not absolute, as the power applies only to the appointment of *principal* not *inferior* officers and is subject to senate approval. Similarly, the Constitution implicitly gives the executive the power to remove officers subject to conditions Congress imposes. This power, therefore, is not absolute. Note, however, that although Congress has the authority to place limits on the executive's removal power, Congress does not have the authority to eliminate that power altogether.[20] We will cover the appointment power more specifically below.

Like formalists, functionalists turn to the vesting clauses of the Constitution to define the most central, core functions of each branch: the legislature legislates, the judiciary adjudicates, and the executive enforces the law. But unlike formalists, functionalists do not compartmentalize these core functions. For example, the legislature's power to make law is a core function. The judiciary, however, also makes law, both by developing common law and by interpreting statutes. Under formalism, this encroachment would likely be sufficient to trigger a separation of powers concern. In contrast, under functionalism, the judiciary's encroachment into a core function of the legislature does not raise concern. To trigger a separation of powers concern under functionalism, one branch would have to *unduly* encroach and aggrandize a core function of another branch.

Functionalists believe that overlap between the branches is practically necessary and even desirable. Functionalists emphasize the need to maintain pragmatic flexibility to respond to the needs of modern government. Indeed, the existence of the administrative system is an example of functionalism.[21]

While both formalism and functionalism share a common goal—to ensure that no one branch acquires too much unilateral power—these approaches go about meeting this goal in different ways. Recall that formalists use a two-step, bright-line-rule approach to categorize acts as legislative, judicial, or executive. In contrast, functionalists use a factors approach, which balances the competing power interests with the pragmatic need for innovation.

---

[19] *Id.*

[20] Bowsher v. Synar, 478 U.S. 714, 725–26 (1986); Myers v. United States, 272 U.S. 52, 126–27 (1926).

[21] *See* Peter B. McCutchen, *Mistakes, Precedent, and The Rise of the Administrative State: Toward a Constitutional Theory of the Second Best*, 80 CORNELL L. REV. 1, 11 (1994) (arguing that "[u]nder a pure formalist approach, most, if not all, of the administrative state is unconstitutional.").

Functionalists recognize the government's need for flexibility to create new power-sharing arrangements to address the evolving needs of the modern century. Functionalists do not want to "unduly constrict Congress's ability to take needed and innovative action . . . ."[22]

To foster flexibility, functionalists focus less on maintaining the separateness of each branch and instead favor the independence of each branch, with oversight from the other branches. This independence is achieved when each branch is able to perform its core functions while also being able to limit the accretion of power by the other branches.

Justice Jackson's tripartite framework from his concurrence in *Youngstown Sheet & Tube Co. v. Sawyer*[23] is informative. Justice Jackson suggested that the Court review separation of powers issues differently, based upon the level of cooperation among the branches. Because the case involved President Truman's seizure of the steel mills, the framework specifically addressed executive power, but the analysis applies to all:

> First, "[w]hen the President acts pursuant to an express or implied authorization of Congress, his authority is at its maximum, for it includes all that he possesses in his own right plus all that Congress can delegate." Second, "[w]hen the President acts in absence of either a congressional grant or denial of authority, he can only rely upon his own independent powers, but there is a zone of twilight in which he and Congress may have concurrent authority, or in which its distribution is uncertain." In such a circumstance, Presidential authority can derive support from "congressional inertia, indifference or quiescence." Finally, "[w]hen the President takes measures incompatible with the expressed or implied will of Congress, his power is at its lowest ebb," and the Court can sustain his actions "only by disabling the Congress from acting upon the subject."[24]

Functionalism can be pictured as a set of interlocking circles, as in the chart below. It contrasts with formalism, which was depicted above as a series of separate circles with no overlap.

---

[22] CFTC v. Schor, 478 U.S. 833, 851 (1986).

[23] 343 U.S. 579 (1952).

[24] Medellin v. Texas, 552 U.S. 491, 494 (2008) (*quoting* Youngstown Sheet & Tube Co. v. Sawyer, 343 U.S. at 635–38 (Jackson, J., concurring)).

FUNCTIONALISM

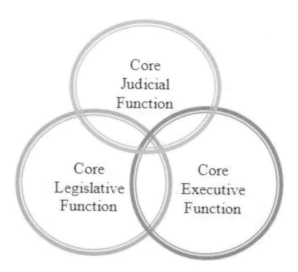

From this chart, it becomes clear that each branch possesses separate, constitutionally assigned, core functions. At the same time, each branch also has a penumbra of overlap (the zone of twilight) that shades gradually into the core functions of the other two branches. So long as the branches steer relatively clear of the other branches' core functions, and so long as the branches do not enlarge the size of their own circle at the expense of another branch's circle, functionalist separation of powers is maintained.

Finally, it is important to know that, while the Founders were indeed concerned about the concentration of governmental power in any one of the three branches, they were primarily concerned with congressional self-aggrandizement. In keeping with this concern, the Court more closely scrutinizes legislation that expands Congress's authority rather than the authority of the other branches. The Court has been more accepting of judicial and executive aggrandizement. Indeed, at least one commentator has suggested that the Court uses formalism when Congress overreaches and uses functionalism when the judiciary or executive overreach.[25]

In summary, functionalists take a pragmatic view of separation of powers and seek to avoid the aggrandizement of a branch at the expense of another branch. Formalists ask what power is being wielded and who is wielding that power. In contrast,

---

[25] Ronald J. Krotoszynski, *On the Danger of Wearing Two Hats: Mistretta and Morrison Revisited*, 38 WM. & MARY L. REV. 417, 460 (1997).

functionalists ask whether one branch has encroached into the core functions of another branch to aggrandize power.

Almost exclusively, when the Court approaches a separation of powers issue under a functionalist approach, the Court approves the exercise of that branch's power.[26] Contrariwise, when the Court approaches a separation of powers issue under a formalist approach, the Court rejects the exercise of that branch's power.[27]

2.   Delegating Legislative & Judicial Power

a.   Delegating Legislative Power

The federal government is a government of limited and enumerated powers; no entity of our government can exercise a power unless the Constitution expressly grants that power to that entity. Article I, § 1 of the U.S. Constitution provides that "All legislative powers herein granted shall be vested in a Congress of the United States . . . ." And Article III, § 1 provides that "all judicial power of the United States shall be vested in one Supreme Court and such inferior courts as the Congress may from time to time ordain and establish." Yet, we know that agencies exercise legislative power when they make general rules. Where do agencies get this power? Certainly not from the Constitution; instead we say that Congress delegates power to the agencies.

Is delegation allowed under the Constitution? The Constitution does not expressly prohibit or allow delegation. Instead, we need to consider a doctrine from agency law, known as the nondelegation doctrine. That doctrine provides that an agent may not subdelegate its power to an assistant. Thus, because a legislature is the agent of the people who elected it, that legislature may not subdelegate its policymaking power to an administrative agency. However, the nondelegation doctrine does permit an agent to tell its assistants how to carry out tasks to accomplish its responsibilities, so long as the agent itself remains in control of the decisions. Thus, under the nondelegation doctrine, Congress can delegate quasi-legislative power to agencies so long as Congress remains in control of the important decisions. In other words, so long as Congress ultimately decides policy, agencies can "fill up the details."[28]

---

[26]   *See, e.g.,* King v. Burwell, 135 S. Ct. 2480, 2496 (2015); Mistretta v. United States, 488 U.S. 361, 368 (1989); *CFTC,* 478 U.S. at 852–56.

[27]   *See, e.g.,* Stern v. Marshall, 564 U.S. 462, 484 (2011); Free Enterprise Fund v. Public Co. Accounting Oversight Bd., 561 U.S. 477, 508 (2010); Plaut v. Spendthrift Farm, Inc., 514 U.S. 211, 240 (1995); *Bowsher,* 478 U.S. at 722–23 (1986); United States v. Klein, 80 U.S. 128, 146 (1871).

[28]   Wayman v. Southard, 23 U.S. 1, 43 (1825).

To determine whether Congress has made the basic policy decision, a court will look to see whether Congress provided an "intelligible principle" in the statute authorizing the agency to act.[29] So long as Congress placed some boundaries on agency authority, delegation is legitimate. If Congress sufficiently and explicitly constrains an agency's policy-making choices, then the agency is not deciding policy; rather, the agency is helping Congress implement the policy it chose. If, however, the delegation is too broad and ambiguous, then the delegation may be unconstitutional. The intelligible principle provides a standard for a court to use to determine whether the agency acted within the "limited" authority Congress delegated to it.

At least the above description is the abstract concept behind the delegation doctrine; however, today, the intelligible principle standard lacks any teeth. The Supreme Court has only struck down three statutes for violating this standard, and all three cases occurred in the 1930s during a time of great turmoil for the United States. During this time, President Franklin Delano Roosevelt came into office promising to turn things around for the American people. Just five days after his election, Congress was called into session and enacted five major pieces of legislation after only forty hours of debate. This rate of speed was unprecedented, and the judiciary's reaction to the power grab was hostile, to say the least. The Supreme Court heard three delegation cases and struck down all of them. Two, the Hot Oil Case[30] and the Sick Chicken Case,[31] involved delegation to agencies; the other involved delegation to third parties.

---

[29]   J.W. Hampton, Jr., & Co. v. United States, 276 U.S. 394, 409 (1928).

[30]   In the first, *Panama Refining Co. v. Ryan*, 293 U.S. 388 (1935), (known as the "Hot Oil case"), the Court struck down a provision of the National Industrial Recovery Act ("NIRA") that allowed the president to prohibit the interstate transportation of oil in excess of that allowed by state law. *Id*. at 420–21. Under the NIRA, Congress wanted to prevent the evasion of strict state laws limiting the amount of oil that oil producers could sell. Striking down the statute, the Court held that Congress did not provide intelligible principles and stated: "As to the transportation of oil production in excess of state permission, the Congress has declared no policy, has established no standard, has laid down no rule. There is no requirement, no definition of circumstances and conditions in which the transportation is to be allowed or prohibited." *Id*. at 430.

[31]   In the second case, *A.L.A. Schechter Poultry Corp. v. United States*, 295 U.S. 495 (1935) (known as the "Sick Chicken case"), the Court struck down another provision in the NIRA that allowed the president to approve codes for "fair competition" that were established jointly with the chicken industry so long as the following conditions were met: (1) the code was written by a representative group of business, (2) the code did not promote monopolies, and (3) the code served goals identified in another section of the NIRA. *Id*. at 538–39. The Court struck down the provision, stating that the President's authority was "virtually unfettered." *Id*. at 541–42.

The delegation to agencies prong of the intelligible principles standard is the piece that lacks teeth today. Since those cases were decided and the President threatened to pack the Supreme Court with his own appointees, the Court adopted a broader view of federal legislative power and never again struck down a statute on delegation grounds. For example, in *Whitman v. American Trucking Ass'n*,[32] the Court reviewed the constitutionality of a section of the Clean Air Act that directed the EPA "to set primary ambient air quality standards 'the attainment and maintenance of which . . . are requisite *to protect the public health.*' "[33] The issue for the Court was whether the language "to protect the public health" sufficiently constrained the delegation; the Court held that it did.[34] Similarly, the Court has held many other broad, vague, and standardless statutes to contain intelligible principles.[35]

In contrast, the third case, *Carter v. Carter Coal Co.*,[36] involved delegation to third parties, namely certain mine owners, to set maximum labor hours. The Court struck down the third party delegation as "legislative delegation in its most obnoxious form; for it is not even delegation to an official or an official body, presumptively disinterested, but to private persons whose interests may be and often are adverse to the interests of others in the same business."[37] This principle—that delegations to third parties are unconstitutional—remains vibrant.

---

[32] 531 U.S. 457 (2001).

[33] *Id.* at 465 (quoting 42 U.S.C. § 7409(b)(1)) (emphasis added).

[34] *Id.* at 472–73.

[35] *See, e.g.*, Touby v. United States, 500 U.S. 160, 167–68 (1991) (upholding as constitutional a law that directed the attorney general to designate certain drugs as controlled substances for purposes of criminal enforcement if doing so was "necessary to avoid an imminent hazard to the public safety") (*quoting* 21 U.S.C. § 811(h)); Industrial Union Dept., ALF-CIO v. American Petroleum Inst., 448 U.S. 607, 639 (1980) (upholding as constitutional a provision in the Occupational Safety and Health Act requiring the agency to "set the standard which most adequately assures to the extent feasible, on the basis of the best available evidence, that no employee will suffer any impairment of health") (*quoting* 29 U.S.C. § 655(b)(6)); American Power & Light Co. v. SEC, 329 U.S. 90, 104 (1946) (upholding as constitutional a statute that allowed the agency to modify the structure of holding company systems to ensure that they are not "unduly or unnecessarily complicate[d]" and do not "unfairly or inequitably distribute voting power among security holders.") (*quoting* Public Utility Act of 1935, 49 Stat. 803). For a general listing of such holdings, see generally, Whitman v. American Trucking Ass'n, Inc., 531 U.S. 457, 474–76 (2001).

[36] 298 U.S. 238 (1936). The statute in the case allowed certain mine owners and miners the authority to set maximum labor hours, which would be binding on other mine owners and miners. *Id.* at 279 (*citing* 15 U.S.C. § 801 to 827 (1935) (repealed in 1937)).

[37] *Id.* at 311.

b. Delegating Judicial Power

The doctrine relating to the delegation of judicial power is much more complicated than the delegation doctrine. Moreover, it has changed over time. Early in this area of jurisprudence, the Supreme Court distinguished between claims involving public and private rights. Public rights involve the liability of the government to its citizens, whereas private rights involve the liability of one individual to another. The Court reasoned that non-Article III courts could adjudicate claims involving public rights because the government does not have to agree to be sued at all under the doctrine of sovereign immunity. If the government does agree to be sued, the government can set the parameters of being sued, including that such adjudication occur before a non-Article III tribunal.[38] "[T]he whole point of the 'public rights' analysis was that no judicial involvement at all was required—executive determination alone would suffice."[39] In contrast, the Court reasoned that claims involving private rights must be heard by an Article III court or at least be subject to Article III judicial review.[40]

But in 1986, the Court appeared to retreat from this private-public rights distinction in *CFTC v. Schor*.[41] The Court allowed the agency to hear a counter-claim that involved purely private rights.[42] Invoking functionalism, the Court explained that the inquiry regarding "the constitutionality of a given congressional delegation of adjudicative functions to a non-Article III body . . . is guided by the principle that practical attention to substance rather than doctrinaire reliance on formal categories should inform application of Article III."[43]

Shor's new functionalist test was short-lived. In *Stern v. Marshall*,[44] the Court revitalized the public-private rights distinction, finding the claim in that case to be purely private and, thus, outside of the bankruptcy courts authority. "[The]

---

[38] Murray's Lessee v. Hoboken Land & Improvement Co., 59 U.S. (18 How.) 272 (1855).

[39] Peter L. Strauss, *The Place of Agencies in Government: Separation of Powers and The Fourth Branch*, 84 COLUM L. REV. 573, 632 (1984).

[40] Northern Pipeline Construct. Co. v. Marathon Pipe Line Co., 458 U.S. 50, 77 (1982) (holding that an Article I court could not hear a purely private claim in bankruptcy); *see* Crowell v. Benson, 285 U.S. 22 (1932) (holding that an agency could constitutionally adjudicate a case involving purely private rights because the agency made only factual findings, which were subject to judicial review by an Article III court).

[41] 478 U.S. 833 (1986).

[42] *Id*. at 847.

[43] *Id*. at 847–48 (internal quotations omitted).

[44] 564 U.S. 462 (2011).

counterclaim . . . does not fall within any of the varied formulations of the public rights exception in this Court's cases . . . . The claim is instead one under state common law between two private parties. It does not 'depend[ ] on the will of congress,' Congress has nothing to do with it . . . ."[45] Justice Scalia put the distinction more clearly:—"a matter of public rights . . . must at a minimum arise between the government and others."[46]

C.   Constitutional Constraints on Appointment & Removal

1.   Overview

The Constitution is also relevant to appointment and removal issues. When Congress creates an agency, Congress must determine the structure of that agency, including the appointment and removal of the agency's officials. In Chapter 1, we learned that one difference between independent and executive agencies is that independent agencies are often headed by multi-member boards, each of whom is appointed with the advice and consent of the Senate[47] and removable only for cause. In contrast, the heads of executive agencies, who are also appointed with the advice and consent of the Senate, generally serve at the president's pleasure, meaning they are removable at will. One issue you should consider is whether the appointment and removal provisions of an enabling statute are constitutional. Appointment challenges and removal challenges often occur together.

Under the Constitution, Congress shares the appointment power with the president in two relevant ways. First, while the president can appoint whomever he or she pleases, the Senate must confirm presidential appointments of principal officers including heads of agencies.[48] Second, Congress has the power to vest the appointment power of "inferior" officers in the president, the courts of law, or in heads of departments.[49]

While   the   Constitution   explicitly   provides   for   the appointment[50] of principal and inferior officers, it does not explicitly

---

[45]   *Id.* at 493 (internal quotations omitted).

[46]   *Id.* at 503 (Scalia, J., concurring) (internal quotations omitted).

[47]   U.S. CONST. art. II § 2 cl. 2.

[48]   *Id.*

[49]   *Id.*

[50]   The Constitution provides that "[t]he executive Power shall be vested in a President of the United States of America." U.S. CONST. art. II, § 1, cl. 1. As Madison stated on the floor of the First Congress, "if any power whatsoever is in its nature Executive, it is the power of appointing, overseeing, and controlling those who execute the laws." 1 Annals of Cong. 463 (1789).

address removal.[51] The Supreme Court has held that the Constitution vests removal power in the president *implicitly* because that power was not " 'expressly taken away' " from the president in the Constitution.[52] And, as it has been with appointment cases, the Court has not provided clear guidance in the removal cases.

The distinctions between (1) principal officers and inferior officers, and (2) inferior officers and employees are relevant to both appointment and removal issues. Unfortunately, the Supreme Court has not offered clear and consistent guidance on the difference between principal officers, inferior officers, and employees. The Court's test has changed with each case it has heard.

2. Appointment

First, let's look at the law regarding appointments. The Appointments Clause of the Constitution describes the permissible methods of appointing "Officers of the United States," a class of government officials that does not include mere employees.[53] The president, with the advice and consent of the Senate appoints *principal* officers, while the president, a court of law, or a head of department can appoint an *inferior* officer.[54] Inferior officers differ from principal officers in that inferior officers have a superior who is below the president.[55]

The line between officer and mere employee is less bright-lined. The Supreme Court has established a two part test for distinguishing between them. Using the first prong of that test, a court examines whether the individual holds a "continuing" position established by law.[56] The position must be "continuing and permanent," rather than "occasional or temporary."[57] This prong of the test is generally easy to resolve.

Using the second prong, a court examines whether the individual exercises significant authority pursuant to the laws of

---

[51] The Constitution contains only one removal provision, which provides that "all civil officers of the United States [may] be removed from office on impeachment for, and conviction of, treason, bribery, or other high crimes and misdemeanors." U.S. CONST. art. II, § 4.

[52] Free Enterprise Fund v. Public Co. Accounting Oversight Bd., 561 U.S. 477, 492 (2010) (*quoting* Letter from James Madison to Thomas Jefferson (June 30, 1789), 16 Documentary History of the First Federal Congress 893 (2004)).

[53] Art. II, § 2, cl. 2.

[54] *Id.*

[55] Edmond v. United States, 520 U.S. 651, 662 (1997).

[56] United States v. Germaine, 99 U.S. 508, 511-12 (1879).

[57] *Id.*

the United States.[58] This prong of the test is more difficult to resolve because the Court has not clearly explained what "significant authority" means.[59] The Court has merely decided the issue in individual cases.

For example, the Court has granted inferior office status to many a lesser functionary, including a district court clerk,[60] a federal marshal,[61] and, special trial judges (STJs) of the United States Tax Court.[62] In the latter case, the Court reasoned that STJs "take testimony, conduct trials, rule on the admissibility of evidence, and have the power to enforce compliance with discovery orders."[63] Moreover, "[i]n the course of carrying out these important functions, [they] exercise significant discretion;"[64] hence, the STJs were officers.[65]

The Court explicitly rejected the government's argument that officials who "lack authority to enter into a final decision" must be employees and not inferior officers because that argument "ignore[d] the significance of the duties and discretion that special trial judges possess."[66] More recently, the Court held that Securities and Exchange ALJs were officers because they exercised powers identical to those of the STJs.[67]

3. Removal

Let's now examine the law regarding removal. The Constitution does not specifically address removal; however, the courts presume the president has such power because it was not expressly withheld. For example, in *Myers v. United States*,[68] the Supreme Court struck down a statute that required the president to obtain the advice and consent of the Senate prior to removing the postmaster general, a principal officer.

But the president's power is not unlimited. Thus, in *Humphrey's Executor v. United States*,[69] the Court upheld a

---

[58]   Buckley v. Valeo, 424 U.S. 1, 126 (1976).

[59]   Lucia v. SEC, 2018 WL 3057893, * at 5 (U.S. June 21, 2018).

[60]   In re Hennen, 38 U.S. (13 Pet.) 230, 258 (1839).

[61]   Ex parte Siebold, 100 U.S. 371, 397 (1879).

[62]   Freytag v. Commissioner, 501 U.S. 868 (1991).

[63]   *Id.,* at 881–882.

[64]   *Id.,* at 882.

[65]   *Id.*

[66]   *Id.* at 881.

[67]   *Lucia,* 2018 WL 3057893, * at 7.

[68]   272 U.S. 52, 106–18, 176 (1926).

[69]   295 U.S. 602, 620 (1935) (quoting The Federal Trade Commission Act, c. 311, 38 Stat. 717; 15 U.S.C. § 1).

provision in the Federal Trade Commission Act that permitted the president to dismiss a commissioner of the Federal Trade Commission (FTC), also a principal officer, only for "inefficiency, neglect of duty, or malfeasance in office." The Court distinguished its holding in *Myers* by noting that the postmaster general performed purely executive functions and had to be responsible to the president while the FTC member performed quasi-legislative or quasi-judicial powers and had to be independent of the president.[70] Thus, the Court limited *Myers*'s holding to "all purely executive officers."[71]

This distinction did not last long. However, in *Morrison v. Olson*,[72] the Court rejected the *Myers/Humphrey*'s distinction as determinative. In *Morrison*, the Court upheld a for-cause removal limitation on a "purely executive" *inferior* officer, an independent counsel. The Court said, "the determination of whether the constitution allows Congress to impose a 'good cause'-type restriction on the [p]resident's power to remove an official cannot be made to turn on whether or not that official is classified as 'purely executive.' "[73] The Court reasoned that the most important question was whether the removal restriction "impedes the [p]resident's ability to perform his Constitutional duty" to ensure that the laws are faithfully executed.[74] The Court then reasoned that because the independent counsel (1) was an inferior officer, (2) had limited jurisdiction, (3) did not have tenure, (4) lacked policymaking power, and (5) did not have significant administrative authority, the for-cause removal provision was a reasonable restriction on the president's removal authority. However, *Morrison*'s rejection of the *Myers/Humphrey*'s distinction was short-lived.

In *Free Enterprise Fund v. Public Co. Accounting Oversight Bd.*,[75] the Court resurrected the distinction to hold that dual for-cause removal provisions are unconstitutional because the president cannot " 'take care the Laws be faithfully executed' if he cannot oversee the faithfulness of the officers who execute them."[76]

---

[70] *Id.* at 627–28. *See also* Weiner v. United States, 357 U.S. 349, 350 (1958) (limiting the [p]resident's ability to remove a Commissioner of the War Claims Commission, which had only a three-year existence, even though the relevant statute was silent regarding removal because Congress intended to insulate the Commission from presidential interference).

[71] *Humphrey's Executor*, 295 U.S. at 628.

[72] 487 U.S. 654, 689 (1988).

[73] *Id.*

[74] *Id.*

[75] 561 U.S. 477, 484 (2010).

[76] *Id.*

In sum, whether an appointment or removal provision is constitutional depends on whether the officer involved is a principal officer, an inferior officer, or an employee and whether the officer exercises core executive power or quasi-judicial or quasi-legislative power. Regardless, removal limitations cannot impede a president's ability to ensure the laws are faithfully executed.

                    AUTHORITY TO ACT CHECKLIST

A. *Statutory Authority*—Does the Agency have *statutory* authority to act?

    1. Does the enabling or another statute authorize the agency to conduct rulemaking, adjudication, or investigation, as applicable?

        a. **No**—If no, the agency has no legal authority to act. Stop here. *Caveat*: Note that an agency does not need statutory authority to announce what its policy is or how it interprets a statute or regulation because such actions do not make law.

        b. **Yes**—If yes, proceed to A.2. below.

    2. Did the agency comply with all additional requirements in the enabling statute, other relevant statutes, and relevant executive orders (*e.g.*, the Regulatory Flexibility Act and E.O. 12,866)?

        a. **No**—If no, the agency must go back and follow these procedures. Stop here.

        b. **Yes**—If yes, proceed to B. below.

B. *Constitutional Authority*—Is the agency's structure constitutional? (Warning, the law in this area is far from settled and does not lend itself to a simple checklist answer).

    1. **Appointment**—Is the relevant actor a principal officer (typically heads of agencies), an inferior officer (those working closely with the heads of agencies), or an employee? Officers hold "continuing" positions established by law and exercise "significant authority." Inferior officers have supervisors.

        a. **Principal Officer**—If the officer is a principal officer, does the enabling statute provide that the president will appoint and the Senate must confirm?

i.   **No**—If no, the statute is unconstitutional, and the officer has no authority to act. <u>Stop here</u>.

ii. **Yes**—If yes, the officer is constitutionally appointed under U.S. CONST. art. II § 2 cl. 2. <u>Proceed to B.2. below</u>.

b. **Inferior Officer**—If the officer is an inferior officer, does the enabling statute vest the appointment power in the president, the courts of law, or in the head of a department?

   i.   **No**—If no, the statute is unconstitutional, and the officer has no authority to act. <u>Stop here</u>.

   ii. **Yes**—If yes, the officer is constitutionally appointed under U.S. CONST. art. II § 2 cl. 2. <u>Proceed to B.2. below</u>.

c. **Employee**—If the officer is an employee, there are no constitutional requirements relating to appointment. Congress can limit the appointment and removal of employees as it wishes. <u>Proceed to B.2. below</u>.

2. **Removal**—Is there any limit on the president's power to remove the relevant actor, such as a for-cause restriction?

a. **No**—If no, then the actor is constitutionally removable under the Constitution because there are no limits on the president's power to remove. <u>Proceed to C. below</u>.

b. **Yes**—If yes, then ask whether the relevant actor is a principal officer, an inferior officer, or an employee? (See above for definitions).

   i.   **Principal Officer**—If the officer is a principal officer, ask whether the officer performs purely executive acts.

      (a). **Executive Acts**—If the officer performs purely executive acts, then any restriction is likely unconstitutional under *Myers*. <u>Stop here</u>.

      (b). **Quasi-Legislative/Adjudicatory Acts**—If the officer performs quasi-legislative/ adjudicatory acts, then the restriction is likely unconstitutional under *Humphrey's Executor*. <u>Proceed to C. below</u>.

    ii. Inferior Officer—If the officer is an inferior officer, then ask whether the president can perform her or his constitutional duty to ensure that the laws are faithfully executed with the removal restriction in place. Generally, single for-cause removal restrictions are constitutional, while dual for-cause removal restrictions are unconstitutional.

        (a). No—If no, then any restriction is likely unconstitutional under *Free Enterprise*. <u>Stop here</u>.

        (b). Yes—If yes, then any restriction is likely constitutional under *Free Enterprise*. <u>Proceed to C. below</u>.

    iii. Employee—If the officer is an employee, then the actor is constitutionally removable under the Constitution. Congress can limit the appointment and removal of employees as it wishes. <u>Proceed to C. below</u>.

C. *Constitutional Authority*—Does the agency have *constitutional* authority to act?

    1. For Rulemaking—Did Congress provide an *intelligible principle* to guide the agency's decisionmaking? Examples of intelligible principles include "requisite to protect the public health," "necessary to avoid an imminent hazard to the public safety," "adequately assures . . . that no employee will suffer any impairment of health," and "[not] unduly or unnecessarily complicate[d]."

        a. No—If no, which is unlikely, the statute is unconstitutional and the agency has no legal authority to act. <u>Stop here</u>.

        b. Maybe—If maybe, consider whether the court should apply the constitutional avoidance doctrine to avoid interpreting the statute in a way that would violate the delegation doctrine. If so, <u>proceed to Chapter 3</u>.

        c. Yes—If yes, the statute is constitutional. <u>Proceed to Chapter 3</u>.

    2. For Adjudication—Does the issue involve public rights, meaning an issue arising between the government and another, or private rights, meaning an issue arising between individuals and entities other than the government?

a. **Private Rights**—If the issue involves only private rights, then the delegation is likely unconstitutional. Stop here.

b. **Public Rights**—If the issue involves public rights, then the delegation is likely constitutional. Proceed to Chapter 4.

3. **For Investigation**—Proceed to Chapter 5.

ILLUSTRATIVE PROBLEMS

■ PROBLEM 2.1 ■

A federal statute authorizes the Secretary of the Food and Drug Administration (FDA) to engage in rulemaking and adjudication to determine which ingredients are "safe for ingestion by children under age 5 for use in the production of infant formula." The FDA promulgated a regulation using notice-and-comment rulemaking prohibiting a particular ingredient from being included in infant formulas, deeming it unsafe. You are general counsel for the manufacturer of that ingredient. The manufacturer wishes to sue the FDA to stop the regulation from taking effect. The manufacturer asks you whether the FDA's action is constitutional. What do you advise?

Analysis

This issue here is whether Congress's delegation to the FDA to engage in rulemaking is constitutional. Using the checklist above (C.1.), you should ask whether Congress provided an *intelligible principle* to guide the agency's decisionmaking? Examples of intelligible principles include "requisite to protect the public health," "necessary to avoid an imminent hazard to the public safety," "adequately assures . . . that no employee will suffer any impairment of health," and "[not] unduly or unnecessarily complicate[d]." Here, the language in the statute is "safe for ingestion by children under age 5 for use in the production of infant formula." This intelligible principle would be sufficient under the Supreme Court's current delegation doctrine to support the agency's rulemaking.

■ PROBLEM 2.2 ■

Your client is the Secretary of the Department of Veterans Affairs (VA). Recently, the VA was involved in a scandal involving patient care. Your client has been getting pressure from the President to resign because he is angry at her handling of the publicity from the event. She would like advice from you regarding whether the President can fire her if she refuses to step down. Assume the relevant statute allows for-cause removal only. What would you advise?

Analysis

This issue here is whether the President has unfettered power to remove the Secretary of the VA. Using the checklist above (B.2.), you would note that the relevant statute has a for-cause limitation; however, it is unclear whether that limitation would be constitutional. You must determine whether the Secretary is a principal officer or an inferior officer. Secretaries of agencies are typically principal officers because they have no superiors between them and the president. Next you must ask what type of functions the Secretary performs. Here, the Secretary performs purely executive functions and heads an executive agency; she does not adjudicate or promulgate rules directly. Hence, any restriction is likely unconstitutional under *Myers v. United States*, 272 U.S. 52, 239 (1926).

POINTS TO REMEMBER

- The statute that creates an agency, authorizes the agency to act, and identifies the agency's agenda is known as the enabling, or organic, statute. It is the first law to search when trying to determine whether an agency had the power to act.

- Other statutes may augment or limit agency powers, such as the Congressional Review Act. Under that Act, agencies must send all new rules to the Comptroller General for review. Rules with economic impacts greater than $100 million are stayed for sixty days.

- Executive orders may place limits on agencies. For example, E.O. 12,866 provides that agencies may promulgate regulations only when they are "required by law," "necessary to interpret the law," or "are made necessary by compelling public need, such as material failures of private markets to protect or improve the health and safety of the public, the environment, or the well-being of the American people."

- The Constitution also limits agency power. Pursuant to the delegation doctrine Congress must provide the agency with an "intelligible principle" in the statute authorizing the agency to exercise quasi-legislative power. The Court has only struck down three statutes for violating this standard, and all three cases occurred during the Great Depression, a time of great turmoil in the United States. The standard for proper delegation of quasi-judicial power is less clear, but relates to the distinction between private and public rights.

- The Constitution places limits on the appointment and removal of agency officials. Principal officers, like agency heads, must be appointed by the president with the advice and consent of the Senate. Inferior officers, like other higher level agency officials, must be appointed by the president, the courts of law, or the head of the department.

- The *formalist* approach to separation of powers emphasizes the necessity of maintaining three distinct branches of government, each with delegated powers: one branch legislates, one branch adjudicates, and one branch executes. These powers come from the vesting clauses of the U.S. Constitution.

- To maintain a relatively balanced power distribution, functionalists believe that a complete bar against any encroachment between the branches is unnecessary. Instead, functionalists focus on limiting encroachments into the core, constitutionally-appointed functions of each branch. Functionalists turn to the vesting clauses of the Constitution to define the most central, core functions of each branch: the legislature legislates, the judiciary adjudicates, and the executive enforces the law.

CHAPTER 3

What Procedures Are Required for Rulemaking?

From Chapter 1, you have learned to identify the type of action first. From Chapter 2, you learned to evaluate the enabling act, other statutes, executive orders, and the Constitution to be sure that the agency has the power to act. From the next three chapters you will learn the appropriate procedures for each of the three types of agency action. In this chapter, you will learn what procedures the APA requires from rulemaking. In Chapters 4 and 5, you will learn the procedures required for adjudication and informational activities respectively.

REVIEW

Assuming an agency has statutory and constitutional authority to issue rules, the agency must issue those rules pursuant to the applicable procedures provided in the APA.

A.   Initiating a Rulemaking

While an agency may choose to begin the rulemaking process, anyone may petition an agency to issue, amend, or repeal a rule.[1] In response, the agency will (1) grant the petition and begin a rulemaking proceeding, (2) deny the petition, or (3) delay ruling on the petition.

If the agency denies the petition, the agency must provide a prompt explanation for its denial.[2] Denial of a petition is subject to judicial review.[3] Typically, courts sustain an agency's denial unless

---

[1]   APA § 553(e) (2012).

[2]   *Id.* In addition, the agency's rules may affect the manner or timing of an agency's response to a citizen's petition, such as requiring the agency to ask for public comment before denying a petition or requiring the agency publish the reasons for denial.

[3]   APA §§ 551(13) & 704 (2012).

the court finds that decision to be arbitrary and capricious.[4] Chapter 7 more fully explains this standard of review; however, an agency's decision to deny a petition is considered to be arbitrary and capricious when the agency either fails to adequately explain the facts and policy concerns leading to its decision or when the facts the agency relied on have no basis in the record.[5] Sometimes Congress requires an agency to issue a rule. If Congress does so, judicial review of the denial may be more demanding.[6]

If, instead of denying the petition, the agency delays ruling on the petition, that delay may violate the APA. The APA requires the agency to respond within a reasonable time: "Prompt notice shall be given of the denial in whole or in part of a written . . . petition."[7] Despite this language, courts are very deferential to agency decisions to delay. Delays of five years have survived judicial review.

Courts apply what is commonly referred to as the TRAC rule of reason test[8] to determine whether a delay is unreasonable. TRAC's four factors are (1) whether Congress provided a timetable for the agency action; (2) whether the delay would negatively affect human health and welfare; (3) whether expediting the delay would lead to negative effects on issues of higher priority for the agency; and (4) whether the nature and extent of other interests would be unduly prejudiced by the delay.[9] The court need not find that the agency acted inappropriately to find that it delayed unreasonably.[10] When a court finds that the agency unreasonably delayed acting on a petition, the court will typically provide the agency with a timeframe within which to respond to the petition rather than ordering an immediate response.[11]

B. Types of Rules & Rulemaking Procedures

Once an agency decides to issue a rule, the agency must decide how to do so. Check the agency's enabling statute first to see if specific procedures are required. In addition to the procedures the enabling act may require, the APA provides default procedures. Specifically, the APA governs an agency's choice regarding which

---

[4]   APA § 706(1)(A) (2012).

[5]   Arkansas Power & Light Co. v. ICC, 725 F.2d 716, 723 (1984).

[6]   *See, e.g.*, Massachusetts v. EPA, 549 U.S. 797, 497 (2007) (reversing the EPA's decision to refuse to act in light of the statutory direction to the agency to act).

[7]   APA § 555(b) (2012).

[8]   Telecommunications Research & Action Ctr. v. FCC, 750 F.2d 70 (D.C. Cir. 1984) ("*TRAC*").

[9]   *Id* at 80.

[10]   *Id.*

[11]   *See* Norton v. South Utah Wilderness Alliance, 542 U.S. 55, 65 (2004).

rulemaking process to follow. Under the APA, agencies may issue rules in one of three ways: formal rulemaking, notice-and-comment rulemaking (also known as informal rulemaking), and publication rulemaking. Below are the different types of rules (legislative and non-legislative) and the corresponding rulemaking procedures.

1. Types of Rules

There are two kinds of rules: (1) legislative rules, and (2) non-legislative rules. Legislative rules have legal (or binding) effect. If a regulated entity violates a legislative rule, the entity will be subject to some form of a penalty. Legislative rules are typically contained in regulations.

Non-legislative rules do not have independent, binding legal effect. Rather, any legal effect they have comes from pre-existing legislative rules (whether from Congress or the agency). Non-legislative rules are often collectively called "guidance documents." There are two kinds of guidance documents: (1) interpretive rules,[12] and (2) general statements of policy.[13] Interpretive rules are rules interpreting language in an existing statute or regulation. In contrast, policy statements are communications that prospectively advise the public and agency personnel on the way in which the agency plans to exercise discretionary power in the future.

2. Types of Rulemaking

The APA sets forth three kinds of rulemaking *procedures*: (1) formal rulemaking, (2) notice-and-comment rulemaking, and (3) publication rulemaking. A fourth form of rulemaking also exists: hybrid rulemaking. The procedures for each are explained below.

a. Formal Rulemaking

Formal rulemaking is relatively rare, in part because the procedures used in this type of rulemaking are better suited for resolving adjudicative facts (*e.g.*, who is telling the truth), rather than for resolving legislative facts (*e.g.*, what degree of arsenic in the soil is safe). Formal rulemaking requires a hearing with civil, trial-like procedures. Entities and individuals whom the rule might impact have a right to notice of the hearing and a right to participate in the hearing in some fashion.[14] The rules of evidence do not apply.[15] A hearing officer, known as an ALJ, compiles the record and makes either an initial decision or recommendation to

---

12   While the APA uses interpretative, interpretive is more commonly used.
13   APA § 553(b)(3)(A) (2012).
14   APA §§ 554(b) & (c) (2012).
15   *See* APA § 556(c)(3) (2012) (instructing ALJs to receive relevant evidence).

the agency head.[16] The agency head then either adopts the ALJ's decision or issues a final decision. That decision is subject to judicial review.[17] These procedures are identical to those the APA requires for formal adjudication.[18] Hence, these procedures are covered in more detail in Chapter 4.

b.   Notice & Comment Rulemaking Procedures

Notice-and-comment (informal) rulemaking is significantly more common. This form of rulemaking is known as notice-and-comment rulemaking because the APA requires an agency to publish notice of its proposed rule in the Federal Register (notice) and to solicit and respond to comments from the public and others about the proposed rule (comment).[19] Let's look at each requirement more carefully.

The APA requires agencies to give adequate notice of the substance of a new rule to provide members of the public an opportunity to comment on the proposed rule. The notice must be "sufficient to fairly apprise interested persons of the issues involved, so that they may present responsive data or argument."[20] The agency must include the time, place, and nature of any public proceedings; the legal authority for the rule; and either the substance of the proposed rule or a description of the subjects and issues involved.[21] Additionally, the D.C. Circuit Court has held that the notice of proposed rulemaking ("NPRM") must include all the scientific data and methodology on which the agency relied.[22] Most agencies today include a final draft of the proposed rule and statements showing their compliance with the requirements other statutes and executive orders impose even though the additional information is not always required to be included.

Any "interested person" can submit "written data, views, or arguments" on a proposed rule.[23] The APA does not require oral commenting, and it is generally not allowed. No fixed time period

---

[16]   APA § 554(d) (2012).

[17]   APA § 706(2) (2012).

[18]   *See* APA §§ 554 (1978) & 556 (2012).

[19]   APA § 553(b) & (c) (2012).

[20]   H.R. Rep. No. 1980, 79th Cong., 2d Sess. 2, reprinted in Legislative History of the Administrative Procedure Act, S. Doc. No. 248, 79th Cong., 2d Sess. 200 (1946).

[21]   APA § 553(b)(1)–(3) (2012).

[22]   Portland Cement Ass'n v. Ruckelshaus, 486 F.2d 375, 394 (D.C. Cir. 1973). Yet this requirement is contrary to the actual language of § 553 and may be invalid under a later Supreme Court case: *Vermont Yankee Nuclear Power Corp. v. Natural Resources Defense Council, Inc.*, 435 U.S. 519, 524 (1978).

[23]   APA § 553(c).

for commenting is required. Typically, the rulemaking record will include all the rulemaking notices, copies of all written factual material the agency substantially relied upon or seriously considered, and all written comments submitted.[24]

The APA does not prohibit ex parte communications for notice-and-comment rulemaking. The Due Process Clause limits ex parte communications when those proceedings involved "conflicting private claims to a valuable privilege."[25] This limitation applies only when the parties are essentially arguing about agency action that results in a property-like award, such as a license. In addition, an agency's own rule or the agency's enabling statute may prohibit ex parte communications.[26]

After the comment period, the agency must "consider" the submitted comments and draft its final rule.[27] With the final rule, the agency must prepare and publish a "concise general statement of [the rule's] basis and purpose."[28]

The final rule need not be identical to the proposed rule to satisfy the APA's notice requirement; which makes sense. If agencies could not change course at all then why have public comment? However, if there is too much change, then the notice may be insufficient to fairly apprise interested persons of the substance of the proposed rule. Courts have sought to ensure that the final rule is close enough to the rule as proposed so as to make the opportunity to comment meaningful. Notice is insufficient if it does not give fair notice of the rule as finally promulgated. If the final rule can be characterized as a "logical outgrowth" of the proposed rule—meaning that the final rule does not materially alters the issues involved in the rulemaking and did not substantially depart from the substance of the proposed rule, then notice was adequate.[29] "Notice [is] inadequate when the interested parties could not reasonably have anticipated the final rulemaking from the draft."[30] Or as one court put it, the agency must avoid the

---

24   *See* Citizens to Preserve Overton Park v. Volpe, 401 U.S. 402, 420 (1971); Home Box Office, Inc. v. FCC, 567 F.2d 9, 54 (D.C. Cir. 1977).

25   Sangamon Valley v. United States, 269 F.2d 221, 224 (D.C. Cir. 1959).

26   *See* Home Box Office Inc. v. FCC, 567 F.2d 9, 56–57 (D.C. Cir. 1977) (analyzing a statute that included a restriction on agency ex parte communications).

27   APA § 553(c).

28   *Id.* Although the language in the APA requires a concise statement, under pressure from the lower courts setting aside rules the courts considered inadequately explained, agencies have acted in preemptive self-defense by crafting lengthy and detailed explanations called preambles.

29   Chocolate Mf., Ass'n v. Block, 755 F.2d 1098, 1105 (4th Cir. 1985).

30   National Mining Ass'n v. MSHA, 116 F.3d 520, 531 (D.C. Cir. 1997).

"surprise switcheroo."[31] The goal of this test is to balance the inconvenience to the agency of having to redo notice-and-comment with the rights of regulated entities to be put on notice that their interests are at stake. In other words, regulated entities should know the issue is on the table.

      c.   Publication Procedures

Publication rulemaking is becoming increasingly common as agency find notice-and-comment rulemaking more cumbersome. The APA allows agencies to avoid both formal rulemaking and notice-and-comment rulemaking altogether when promulgating specific kinds of rules.[32] The specific kinds of rules for which publication procedures can be used are detailed below. The publication procedures themselves are explained here.

Publication rulemaking is significantly easier than notice-and-comment rulemaking. Indeed, all an agency need do is publish the rule in the Federal Registrar (as opposed to the Code of Federal Registrar, where agencies publish legislative rules) or provide the entity to be regulated with actual notice.[33] Then, these rules typically take effect no sooner than thirty days after they are promulgated.[34] That is it.

      d.   Hybrid Procedures

As noted in Chapter 2, Congress may add additional procedures in either the enabling act or in another statute.[35] And the president may do so in an executive order.[36] Further, agencies may require additional procedures of themselves.[37] Congress, the president, and even agencies can impose additional rulemaking

---

[31] Environmental Integrity Project v. EPA, 425 F.3d 992, 997 (D.C. Cir. 2005).

[32] APA § 553 (b).

[33] APA § 552(1) (Supp. 2016). Alternatively, the agency may provide actual notice to anyone against whom the agency wishes to enforce a rule. *See e.g.*, United States v. F/V Alice Amanda, 987 F.2d 1078, 1084 (4th Cir. 1993) (holding that lack of publication was harmless error when person had actual notice of the rule).

[34] APA § 553(d) (2012).

[35] For example, the Regulatory Flexibility Act requires agencies to create a Regulatory Flexibility Analysis for any proposed rule that will significantly impact a substantial number of small businesses, organizations, or governments. 5 U.S.C. § 601 *et seq.* (2012). And the Unfunded Mandates Reform Act requires agencies to prepare a statement assessing the effect of any proposed regulation that will cause state, local, or tribal governments to incur more than $100 million annually. 2 U.S.C. § 1501 *et seq.* (2012).

[36] *See, e.g.*, E.O. 12,866, 58 Fed. Reg. 51735 (1993) (requiring agencies to conduct a cost-benefit analysis on all proposed rules that are "significant.").

[37] *Cf.* APA § 553(b)(3)(A) (exempting agency procedural rules from notice-and-comment requirements).

procedures to those the APA requires. Rulemaking involving additional procedures is typically known as hybrid rulemaking. Importantly, however, the Supreme Court has held that courts cannot require more procedure than that required by the APA, the Constitution, or a statute.[38] Thus, the APA is the starting point for procedural requirements, not the ending point.

3. Summary of Types of Rules & Rulemaking

The flowchart below shows the types of rules and rulemaking available to agencies.

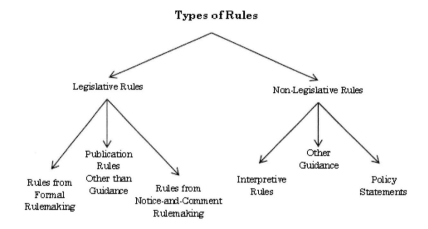

Types of Rules

C. Choosing the Appropriate Rulemaking Procedure

Which form of rulemaking must an agency use? It depends. You may need to examine whether the agency used notice-and-comment rulemaking when the APA or enabling statute required formal rulemaking. Alternatively, you may need to examine whether the agency used publication rulemaking when the APA or enabling statute required notice-and-comment rulemaking. The APA's requirements are explained next.

1. Formal Rulemaking v. Notice & Comment Rulemaking

The APA requires agencies to use formal rulemaking, rather than notice-and-comment rulemaking, only "[w]hen rules are required by statute to be made on the record after opportunity for an agency hearing . . . ."[39] The agency has the power to interpret language in its enabling statute to decide whether Congress

---

[38] Vermont Yankee Nuclear Power Corp. v. Natural Resource Defense Council, Inc., 435 U.S. 519, 524 (1978).

[39] APA § 553(c).

intended for the agency to use formal or notice-and-comment procedures.[40] The Supreme Court held that agencies must use formal rulemaking only when the enabling statute requires both a hearing *and* that the hearing be on the record.[41] Thus, courts will typically defer to an agency's interpretation that notice-and-comment procedures are all that is required. In the absence of such "magic language," an agency may use notice-and-comment rulemaking, as augmented by any hybrid requirements from sources other than the APA.

2.   Notice & Comment Rulemaking v. Publication Rulemaking

The APA requires agencies to use notice-and-comment rulemaking, rather than publication rulemaking, for most rules. However, the APA allows an agency to use publication procedures for some kinds of rules. For example, an agency may use publication procedures for the following types of rules: (1) rules relating to military and foreign affairs; (2) rules relating to agency management and personnel; (3) rules relating to public property, loans, grants, benefits, and contracts; (4) rules for which the agency has a "good cause" reason to avoid notice-and-comment rulemaking; and (5) rules of agency organization and practice.[42] An agency's choice to use publication procedures for these types of rules is rarely challenged. You are unlikely to be tested on this topic.

In addition, an agency may use publication procedures to issue procedural rules, good cause rules, interpretive rules, and policy statements.[43] You are more likely to get tested on these exceptions to notice-and-comment rulemaking, so let's explore each and when the agency's choice to use them is valid.

First, procedural rules: the APA allows agencies to use publication procedures for "rules of agency organization, procedure, or practice."[44] Rules of agency organization and practice are generally not challenged. In contrast, rules of agency procedure are more commonly challenged. The APA does not define rules of agency procedure. Most courts distinguish between procedural rules and substantive rules based on whether the rule has a substantial

---

[40]   Dominion Energy Brayton Point v. Johnson, 443 F.3d 12, 16 (1st Cir. 2006) (applying *Chevron* to an agency's determination regarding whether formal or informal adjudication procedures were required).

[41]   United States v. Florida East Coast R.R., 410 U.S. 224, 238 (1973) (holding that a statute that required the agency to issue a rule "after a hearing" did not trigger formal rulemaking); United States v. Allegheny-Ludlum Steel Corp., 406 U.S. 742, 757 (1972) (same).

[42]   APA §§ 553(a), (b)(3)(A) & (b)(3)(B) (2012).

[43]   APA § 553(b)(3)(A).

[44]   *Id.*

impact on the rights of people affected.[45] Rules that have a substantial impact on the parties must be promulgated via notice-and-comment rulemaking.

However, the D.C. Circuit rejected the substantive impact test, claiming that even rules that are clearly procedural affect substantive rights. Instead, this circuit examines whether the rule encodes a substantive value judgment and substantially alters the rights of the parties; if so, notice-and-comment rulemaking is required.[46]

Second, good cause rules: the APA allows agencies to use publication procedures when the agency has good cause to believe that notice would be impracticable, unnecessary, or contrary to the public interest.[47] The agency must include the basis for the good cause exception in its final rule.[48] Although this exception was meant to be a narrow one, agencies often find good cause when none exists.

Third, interpretive rules: the APA allows agencies to use publication procedures when issuing non-legislative interpretive (interpretative) rules. Interpretive rules are self-describing; they are rules interpreting language in an existing statute or regulation. An agency may issue an interpretive rule using formal rulemaking, notice-and-comment rulemaking, or publication rulemaking. However, an agency's choice of publication rulemaking is valid only if the interpretive rule is non-legislative in nature.

In *American Mining Congress v. MSHA*,[49] the D.C. Circuit explained that whether a rule is a legislative or non-legislative interpretive rule depends on whether the agency's intended to exercise its legislative rulemaking powers (the intent to exercise test).

The intent to exercise test has four factors. First, if the basis for agency enforcement of the "interpretive rule" would be inadequate without an existing legislative rule, then the agency likely intended to use its legislative rulemaking authority. Second, if the agency published the "interpretive rule" in the Code of Federal Regulations rather than the Federal Registrar, then the agency likely intended to use its legislative rulemaking authority. Third, if the agency explicitly invoked its legislative rulemaking authority when it issued the "interpretive rule," then the agency

---

[45]   American Hospital v. Bowen, 834 F.2d 1037, 1061–62 (D.C. Cir. 1987).

[46]   JEM Broadcasting Co., Inc. v. FCC, 22 F.3d 320, 328 (D.C. Cir. 1994).

[47]   APA § 553(b)(3)(B).

[48]   APA § 553(b)(3)(B).

[49]   512 F.3d 696, 700 (D.C. Cir. 2008).

likely intended to use its legislative rulemaking authority. Fourth, if the rule repudiates, is irreconcilable with, or otherwise effectively amends a prior legislative rule, the agency likely intended to use its legislative rulemaking authority. If any of these factors are present, then the rule is legislative not non-legislative, and the agency cannot use publication procedures.

Fourth, policy statements: the APA allows agencies to use publication procedures when issuing a policy statement. Policy statements are statements from an agency that advise the public and agency personnel prospectively on the way in which the agency plans to exercise *discretionary* power in the future. Agencies may issue policy statements to announce new duties the agency plans to adopt by future adjudication or rulemaking. To determine whether a rule is a valid policy statement for which an agency may use publication procedures, courts apply the "binding effects" test. Under this test, a rule is a legislative rule rather than a non-legislative policy statement if the rule imposes rights and obligations or restricts an agency's ability to exercise its discretion. Additionally, courts consider whether the agency characterized the rule as legislative or non-legislative; however, this latter factor is not determinative. If these factors are present, then the rule is legislative not non-legislative, and the agency cannot use publication procedures.

  PROCEDURES REQUIRED FOR
RULEMAKING: CHECKLIST

A. **Initiating Rulemaking**—Who initiated the rulemaking?

1. Did a citizen petition to issue, amend, or repeal a rule?

   a. **No**—If no, then there is no agency action until the petition is granted, denied, or ignored. Stop here.

   b. **Yes**—If yes, proceed to A.2. below.

2. Did the agency grant the petition and initiate rulemaking?

   a. **No**—If the petition was not granted, then the agency either denied or delayed acting on the petition. Proceed to A.3. below.

   b. **Yes**—If yes, then you will need to evaluate the agency's choice of rulemaking procedure. Proceed to B. below.

3. Did the agency delay acting on the petition?

    a. **No**—If there is no delay at this time, then the agency must have denied the petition. <u>Proceed to A.4. below</u>.

    b. **Yes**—If yes, then the agency's delay is subject to judicial review under TRAC's rule of reason test. Evaluate (1) whether Congress provided a timetable for the agency action; (2) whether the delay negatively affects human health and welfare; (3) whether expediting the delay would lead to negative effect on issues of higher priority for the agency; and (4) whether the nature and extent of other interests would be unduly prejudiced by the delay. Courts are very deferential of agency decisions to delay. <u>Stop here</u>.

4. Did the agency deny the petition?

    a. **No**—If no, then the agency must have either granted the petition or delayed acting on it. <u>Return to A.2. & A.3. above</u>.

    b. **Yes**— If the petition was denied, then the denial is agency action subject to judicial review. <u>Proceed to the checklists in Chapters 6 and 7</u> to see whether judicial review is available and whether the agency's decision was valid. <u>Stop here</u>.

B. **Choice of Rulemaking Procedure**—Did the agency use the appropriate procedure?

1. Did the agency use notice-and-comment rulemaking or publication rulemaking procedures when it was required to use formal rulemaking procedures?

    a. Did the enabling statute include the phrase "on the record after a hearing" or similar words?

        i. **No**—If no, then the agency could choose to use formal rulemaking procedures but was not required to do so under the APA unless the enabling statute otherwise specifically required formal procedures. The court will apply *Chevron* analysis to evaluate the agency's choice (see Chapter 7).

           (a). If the agency used publication rulemaking procedures, <u>proceed to B.2. below</u>.

           (b). If the agency used notice-and-comment rulemaking procedures, <u>proceed to C. below</u>.

        ii.   **Yes**—If yes, then the agency was required to use formal rulemaking procedures, and its decision not to is invalid. <u>Stop here.</u>

2.   Did the agency use publication rulemaking procedures when it was required to use notice-and-comment rulemaking procedures?

    a.   Does the rule relate to (1) to military and foreign affairs; (2) to agency management and personnel, or (3) to public property, loans, grants, benefits, and contracts?

        i.   **No**—If no, then the rule may still be exempt from notice-and-comment rulemaking procedures. <u>Proceed to B.2.b. below</u>.

        ii.   **Yes**—If yes, then the agency was not required to use notice-and-comment rulemaking procedures (unless the enabling statute expressly so provided). The rule is valid. <u>Proceed to C. below</u>.

    b.   Did the agency have good cause to believe that notice would be impracticable, unnecessary, or contrary to the public interest?

        i.   **No**—If no, then the rule may still be exempt from notice-and-comment rulemaking procedures. <u>Proceed to B.2.c. below</u>.

        ii.   **Yes**—If yes, then the agency was not required to use notice-and-comment rulemaking procedures because it has "good cause" to skip those procedures (unless the enabling statute expressly so provided). The rule is valid. <u>Proceed to C. below</u>.

    c.   Is the rule a procedural rule, which does not have a substantial impact on the rights of the people affected by it (or, if in D.C., does the rule encode a substantial value judgment)[50]?

        i.   **No**—If no, then the rule may still be exempt from notice-and-comment rulemaking procedures. <u>Proceed to B.2.d. below</u>.

---

[50] The D.C. Circuit applies a different test. It examines whether the rule encodes a substantive value judgment and substantially alters the rights of the parties; if so, notice-and-comment procedures are necessary. JEM Broadcasting Co., Inc. v. FCC, 22 F.3d 320, 328 (D.C. Cir. 1994).

      ii.   **Yes**—If yes, then the agency was not required to use notice-and-comment rulemaking procedures (unless the enabling statute expressly so provided). The rule is valid. <u>Proceed to C. below</u>.

  d. Does the rule *prospectively* advise the public and agency personnel on the way in which the agency plans to exercise *discretionary* power in the future?

      i.   **No**—If no, then the rule likely imposes rights and obligations or restricts agency's ability to exercise its discretion (binding effects test). It is not a valid policy statement, exempt from notice-and-comment rulemaking; however, another exception to notice-and-comment rulemaking may apply. <u>Proceed to B.2.e. below</u>.

      ii.   **Yes**—If yes, then the rule is a non-legislative rule, specifically a policy statement, for which the agency was not required to use notice-and-comment rulemaking (unless the enabling statute expressly so provided). The rule is valid. <u>Proceed to C. below</u>.

  e. Does the rule interpret language in an existing statute or regulation?

      i.   **No**—If no, then either you made a mistake or the rule is a legislative rule, and the agency was required to use notice-and-comment rulemaking procedures. The rule is invalid. <u>Stop here</u>.

      ii.   **Yes**—If yes, then determine whether the agency intended to exercise legislative rulemaking authority. Determine whether the "intent to exercise" factors are present: (1) must the agency refer to an existing legislative rule to enforce the new rule; (2) is the new rule published in the Code of Federal Regulations; (3) did the agency invoke its legislative rulemaking authority to issue the new rule; or (4) is the new rule inconsistent with a prior legislative rule. Are any of the four "intent to exercise" factors are present?

         (a). **No**—If no, then the rule is a non-legislative, interpretive rule, for which the agency was not required to use notice-and-comment rulemaking (unless the enabling statute expressly so provided). The rule is valid. Proceed to C. below.

(b). Yes—If yes, then the agency likely intended to use its legislative rulemaking authority and should not have used publication procedures. The rulemaking process was invalid. Stop here.

C. Rulemaking Procedures—Did the agency follow the appropriate procedures?

 1.   Did the agency use publication procedures?

  a.   No—If no, then the agency used either notice-and-comment rulemaking or formal rulemaking procedures (with hybrid procedures). Proceed to C.2. below.

  b.   Yes—If yes, and the agency published the rule or provided personal notice to the relevant entity, the rule is valid. Stop here.

 2.   Did the agency use notice-and-comment rulemaking procedures?

  a.   Did the *notice* include the time, place, and nature of any public proceedings; the legal authority for the rule; and either the substance of the proposed rule or a description of the subjects and issues involved? Was the notice "sufficient to fairly apprise interested persons of the issues involved, so that they may present responsive data or argument"?[51]

   i.   No—If no, then the notice was insufficient. Stop here.

   ii. Yes—If yes, then the notice was sufficient. Proceed to C.2.b.

  b.   Did the agency engage in ex parte communications during the rulemaking process?

   i.   No—If no, then proceed to C.2.c. Generally, ex parte communications are not prohibited for notice-and-comment rulemaking.

   ii. Yes—If yes, ask whether the rulemaking proceeding involved "conflicting private claims to

_____

[51] The D.C. Circuit also requires the notice contain all the scientific data and methodology on which the agency relied. Portland Cement Ass'n v. Ruckelshaus, 486 F.2d 375, 394 (D.C. Cir. 1973).

a valuable privilege," like a license. If so, the ex parte communications violated the Due Process Clause of the Fifth Amendment and the rulemaking is invalid. If not, <u>proceed to C.2.c.</u> Generally, ex parte communications are not prohibited for notice-and-comment rulemaking.

    c.   Did the agency allow interested parties to submit "written data, views, or arguments" on the proposed rule?

        i.   **No**—If no, then the comment process was insufficient, and the rule is invalid. <u>Stop here</u>.

        ii.   **Yes**—If yes, then the comment opportunity was sufficient. <u>Proceed to C.2.d.</u>

    d.   Did the agency follow any hybrid procedures as required by the enabling statute, the agency's regulations, or other statutes? Note that a court cannot require additional procedures under *Vermont Yankee*.

        i.   **No**—If no, then the rulemaking process was insufficient and the rule is invalid. <u>Stop here</u>.

        ii.   **Yes** If yes, then the rulemaking process was valid. <u>Proceed to C.2.e.</u>

    e.   Can the final rule be characterized as a "logical outgrowth" of the proposed rule, meaning that the final rule did not materially alter the issues involved in the rulemaking and the final rule did not substantially depart from the substance of the proposed rule (there were no surprise switcheroos)?

        i.   **No**—If no, then the notice was insufficient. <u>Stop here</u>.

        ii.   **Yes**—If yes, then the notice was sufficient, and the final rule was validly promulgated. <u>Proceed to the checklists in Chapters 6 and 7</u> to see if the substance of the rule is valid and can be challenged in court.

3.   Did the agency use formal rulemaking procedures?

    a.   **No**—If no, you have reached a wrong answer at some point in your analysis. <u>Start over</u>.

    b.   **Yes**—If yes, then <u>proceed to the checklist in Chapter</u> <u>4</u> to determine whether the agency correctly followed the formal rulemaking requirements.

ILLUSTRATIVE PROBLEMS

■ PROBLEM 3.1 ■

Assume that the National Park Service (NPS) promulgated a regulation banning the use of off-road vehicles in national parks. The enabling statute requires the NPS to promulgate rules "after hearing." The NPS promulgates its regulation using notice-and-comment rulemaking procedures. The NPS's final rule, along with a general statement of basis and purpose, was just published. You work for an association that promotes the interests of snowmobilers and off-road recreation vehicle owners. You have been asked whether the NPS used proper procedures in promulgating its new regulation. What do you advise?

Analysis

This issue here is whether the NPS must use formal rulemaking procedures or may use notice-and-comment procedures. Using the checklist above (B.1.), you should ask whether the agency used notice-and-comment rulemaking when it was required to use formal rulemaking procedures. To answer this question, you would look to see whether the enabling statute includes the phrase "on the record after a hearing" or similar words. *Unites States v. Florida Coast Railroad Co.*, 410 U.S. 224, 234–35 (1973).

The NPS's enabling statute requires only that the NPS promulgate rules "after hearing." This language is insufficient to trigger formal rulemaking. Thus, the NPS could choose to use formal rulemaking procedures but was not required to do so unless the enabling statute specifically required formal procedures.

■ PROBLEM 3.2 ■

Marijuana is becoming a big business in the United States. To help promote the marijuana producing industry, coordinate state laws, and protect consumers, Congress enacted the Marijuana Trade Commission Act (MTCA). The Act creates the Marijuana Trade Commission (the Commission), an independent agency. The Commission is authorized to proceed by adjudication and rulemaking to further the purposes of the Act. The Act directs the Commission to "promulgate rules as necessary to further the public interest."

You are general counsel to the Commission, which wants to promulgate a rule limiting the volume of marijuana retailers can sell to one consumer. The enabling statute does not have relevant language. The Chair of the Commission, who is not a lawyer, would like to issue the rule without using notice-and-comment procedures. He has asked you whether this type of rulemaking fits within any of the APA § 553(b) exceptions. What do you advise?

Analysis

This issue here is whether the Commission can choose not to use notice-and-comment rulemaking under APA § 553 and just use publication procedures. Because the enabling statute contains no relevant language, the APA default rules control. Using the checklist above (B.2.), you should conclude first that the rule does not relate to (1) to military and foreign affairs; (2) to agency management and personnel, or (3) to public property, loans, grants, benefits, and contracts. Therefore, this exception does not apply.

Second, you should conclude that the Commission does not have cause to believe that notice would be impracticable, unnecessary, or contrary to the public interest, so the good cause exception does not apply. Third, you would conclude that this rule is not procedural; it would have a substantial impact on the rights of those affected (or, if in D.C., it encodes a substantive value judgment). Hence, the procedural exception does not apply.

Fourth, you should conclude that the rule does not prospectively advise the public and Commission personnel on the way the Commission plans to exercise discretionary power in the future. Rather, the rule is meant to bind the industry immediately; it imposes rights and obligations and restricts the Commission's ability to exercise its discretion. It does not *prospectively* advise the public and agency personnel on the way in which the agency plans to exercise *discretionary* power in the future. Hence, it is not policy statement, exempt from notice-and-comment rulemaking.

Fifth, and finally, you should conclude that the rule does not appear to interpret language in an existing statute or regulation, although it would be helpful to have more of the enabling statute to confirm this point. Assuming the rule does not interpret any such language, the rule is a legislative rule, and the Commission must use notice-and-comment rulemaking procedures.

POINTS TO REMEMBER

- There are three types of rulemaking procedures: formal, informal, and hybrid. Formal rulemaking is rare and resembles formal adjudication under sections 556 & 557. Hence, it is addressed in the next chapter.

- Most rulemaking is informal rulemaking under section 553. This section contains the minimum rulemaking procedures required, known as notice-and-comment procedures.

- A court will evaluate an agency's choice regarding whether to proceed by formal or informal rulemaking by applying *Chevron*'s two-step standard, which is explained in Chapter 7.

- Congress is increasingly adding procedures in addition to the section 553 procedures to produce rulemaking that is less than formal but more than informal rulemaking; we call rulemaking with additional procedures hybrid rulemaking.

- Rules regarding military and foreign affairs functions and internal management activities are exempt from all of the section 553 requirements.

- Interpretive rules, policy statements, rules of procedure, and good cause rules are exempt from the notice-and-comment requirements of section 553 but remain subject to the publication requirements.

- While agencies may initiate rulemaking on their own, citizens may also petition an agency to promulgate a rule. If the agency denies the petition or unreasonably delays making a decision on the petition, the citizen may file suit.

- Ex parte communications are not prohibited during informal rulemaking because agency officials are acting more like legislators than like judges. The exception is when the proceeding involves conflicting claims to a valuable privilege.

- Executive orders, other statutes, and an agency's own procedural rules may augment the minimal rulemaking procedures in the APA. Under *Vermont Yankee*, courts may not add procedures beyond those that come from these sources.

CHAPTER 4

What Procedures Are Required for Adjudication?

In the last chapter, you learned the procedures the APA requires an agency to follow when it engages in rulemaking. This chapter will explain the procedures the APA requires an agency to follow when it engages in adjudication. While some of these procedures are similar to those for rulemaking, especially formal rulemaking, many more are different. Chapter 5 will address the procedural requirements for informational activities.

REVIEW

Assuming an agency has statutory and constitutional authority to adjudicate, the agency must do so pursuant to the applicable procedures provided in the APA and in conformity with the Due Process Clause of the Federal Constitution.

A. Orders and Adjudications

While there are three types of rules, there is only one type of order. However, there are two types of procedures. Agencies may issue orders using formal adjudication or informal adjudication. The APA governs an agency's choice regarding which adjudication process to follow, although the enabling statute may require an agency to use additional procedures. If so, the enabling statute would apply rather than the APA. Below are the procedures for the different types of adjudicatory procedures.

1. Choosing the Appropriate Adjudication Procedure

Agencies generally prefer to act informally because the law requires so few procedures for informal adjudication. Whether an agency must use formal instead of informal procedures is question of statutory interpretation. To determine whether an agency should have used formal adjudication procedures when it adjudicated a case, a court will look at the language of the enabling statute and the agency's interpretation of that language. The court will apply a deference standard known as the *Chevron*[1] two-step, pursuant to which a court will determine first whether Congress was clear as to which type of hearing was required, and if not, the court will determine second whether the agency's interpretation of the language was reasonable.[2] You can assume that unless Congress included the magic language from APA § 554(a) in the enabling statute—"on the record after opportunity for an agency hearing"— an agency's decision to use informal adjudication procedures was valid.

B.   Formal Adjudication and Rulemaking Procedures

Recall that the APA requires the same procedures for formal rulemaking and adjudication. Because formal procedures are more typically used during adjudication, we delayed identifying them until now.

1.   Notice

First, agencies must notify "[p]ersons entitled to notice of an agency hearing" of where and when the hearing will occur.[3] The APA does not define who is entitled to notice; rather, other statutes and the Due Process Clause of the Constitution identify these persons. The APA requires the agency to give all interested parties the opportunity to submit facts, arguments, and offers of settlement so long as time and the public interest permit it.[4]

Assuming notice is required, the notice must be timely and identify the matters of fact alleged, the relevant law and legal authority, and the agency's jurisdiction to hold the hearing.[5] Notice is adequate when it is complete enough, or sufficient, to fairly apprise interested parties of an agency action that will affect their interests.[6] In other words, notice is sufficient when the regulated entity knows what it did wrong and can respond to the allegations.[7]

---

    1   Chevron U.S.A., Inc. v. Natural Resources Defense Council, Inc., 467 U.S. 837 (1984).

    2   Dominion Energy v. Johnson, 443 F.3d 12, 16 (1st Cir. 2006) (overruling an earlier case establishing a presumption in favor of formal adjudication); Chemical Waste Management, Inc. v. EPA, 873 F.2d 1477, 1482 (D.C. Cir. 1989) (applying *Chevron*).

    3   APA § 554(b) (2012).

    4   APA § 554(c) (2012).

    5   APA § 554(b).

    6   NLRB v. Local Union No. 25, 586 F.2d 959, 961 (2d Cir. 1978); Southwest Sunsites, Inc. v. FTC, 785 F2d 1431, 1435 (9th Cir. 1986).

    7   *See, e.g.,* John D. Copanos & Sons, Inc. v. FDA, 854 F.2d 510, 521 (D.C. Cir. 1988) (holding that notice was sufficient despite coming "perilously close to . . .

The APA grants *parties* the right to appear in person in an agency proceeding by or with counsel or another duly qualified representative.[8] Also, any person who is compelled to appear in person before an agency, as a witness for example, is also entitled to counsel.[9]

2.   The Hearing

The proponent of a rule or order, usually the agency, has the burden of proof.[10] For an administrative hearing, burden of proof includes both the burden of production and the burden of persuasion.[11]

The federal rules of evidence do not apply in administrative hearings. Hearsay is admissible; however, the agency's factual findings must be supported by "substantial evidence."[12] Hearsay evidence alone can be "substantial evidence" within the meaning of the APA judicial review provisions, but it likely has to be the kind of hearsay that is reliable, such as medical reports.[13] Parties in formal adjudications have a right to present their cases personally, to present rebuttal evidence, and to conduct cross-examination *if necessary*.[14] There is no absolute right to cross-examination.[15]

For claims seeking benefits, for applications for initial licenses, and for formal rulemakings, an agency may limit oral testimony, requiring the parties submit relevant information in writing.[16]

3.   The Presiding Officer

One of three individuals must preside at the hearing: (1) the agency, (2) one or more members of the body which comprises the

---

denying the applicant a meaningful opportunity to respond" to the agency's allegations).

[8]   APA § 555(b) (2012).

[9]   *Id.*

[10]   APA § 556(d) (2012).

[11]   Director, OWCP v. Greenwich Collieries, 512 U.S. 267, 279 (1994).

[12]   APA §§ 556(d) & 706(2)(E) (2012).

[13]   *Compare* Consolidated Edison v. NLRB, 305 U.S. 197, 229–30 (1938) (holding that there must be at least a residuum of "competent," non-hearsay evidence in the record to support an order), *with* Richardson v. Perales, 402 U.S. 389, 410 (1971) (upholding an order based entirely on uncorroborated hearsay in the form of a written report from standard and routine medical examinations made by a trained professional).

[14]   APA § 556(d).

[15]   Citizens Awareness Network v. United States, 391 F.3d 338, 351 (1st Cir. 2004) (holding that a party seeking cross-examination had the burden to show that cross was required for a "full and true disclosure of the facts.").

[16]   APA § 556(d).

agency, or (3) one or more ALJs.[17] Most commonly ALJs preside, and they have powers similar to that of a judge.[18]

The ALJ is an employee of the agency he or she serves, but ALJs have some independence from the agency. ALJs can be removed only for cause or due to a reduction in workforce.[19] Additionally, ALJ compensation is determined based on length of service, rather than on performance evaluations.[20]

ALJs are not neutral in the way that an Article III judge is neutral; ALJs are agency employees and must further the agency's substantive mission.[21] However, ALJs are supposed to be impartial.[22] Hence, a litigant may seek to disqualify a biased ALJ by filing an affidavit with the agency.

4. Separation of Functions

The federal Constitution does not prohibit agencies from being investigator, prosecutor, and fact-finder all in one.[23] However, the APA requires agencies to separate employees based on function, meaning that the agency officials who perform investigative or prosecutorial functions cannot supervise or oversee an ALJ.[24] Further, agency prosecutors and investigators cannot participate or advise an ALJ in the decision of the case or in the internal review of the case except as witnesses or counsel in the actual hearing.[25]

One caveat: when the agency or a member or members of the body comprising the agency is deciding the case rather than an ALJ, the separation of functions provision does not apply because investigating and prosecuting are functions agency officials are conducting in the administrator's name and with the administrator's delegated authority.[26]

---

[17]   APA § 556(b) (2012).

[18]   APA § 556(c) (2012).

[19]   5 U.S.C. § 7521 (2012).

[20]   *See generally* 5 U.S.C. § 5372 (2012); 5 U.S.C. § 4301(2)(D) (Supp. 2016).

[21]   *See, e.eg,* FTC v. Cement Inst., 333 U. S. 683, 726–27 (1948) (noting a court's comparative lack of familiarity and experience with an agency's mission).

[22]   APA § 556(b).

[23]   Withrow v. Larkin, 421 U.S. 35, 49–50 (1975).

[24]   APA § 554(d)(2) (2012)

[25]   APA § 554(d)(2). This restriction applies not only to the specific case but also to any "factually related" cases, meaning different cases arising out of the same set of facts.

[26]   APA § 554(d)(2)(C) (2012). Also, the separation of functions prohibition does not apply in two situations: (1) proceedings involving applications for initial licenses, and (2) proceedings involving the validity or application of rates, facilities, or practices of public utilities or carriers. APA § 554(d)(2)(B)–(C) (2012). Proceedings for initial licensing often turn on general, policy considerations (do we need another nuclear reactor?) rather than on contested facts (is this applicant for a license

5.   Ex Parte Communications

Ex parte communications are communications not on the public record and to which notice to all parties was not given.[27] Status reports are not ex parte communications.[28]

There is a difference between ex parte communications and *prohibited* ex parte communications. The APA prohibits some forms of ex parte communications in formal adjudications and rulemakings but allows ex parte communications in informal adjudications and rulemakings. Because the APA does not limit ex parte communications in either informal adjudication or informal rulemaking, any limits that do exist come from another statute, an agency procedural rule, or the Due Process Clause.[29]

For formal hearings, an ALJ cannot discuss *facts is dispute* in a case with *anyone* inside or outside the agency, except in the presence of all other parties.[30] There are three exceptions to this prohibition: (1) proceedings involving applications for initial licenses; (2) proceedings involving the validity or application of rates, facilities, or practices of public utilities or carriers; and (3) proceedings involving the agency or a member or members of the body comprising the agency as the decision maker.[31] Thus, the agency head may communicate with agency staff when making a decision in a case.

Additionally, the decision maker (including the agency and agency head) cannot discuss *the merits of the case* with *interested persons* outside the agency.[32] "Interested persons" includes not only the parties to the case but also anyone who has an interest in the proceeding that is greater than the interest a general member of the public would have.[33] The three exceptions that apply to ex parte

---

qualified?). For this reason, the separation of functions limits are unnecessary. The second exception applies to proceedings involving the validity or application of rates, facilities, or practices of public utilities and carriers. Because the APA includes ratemaking as a form of rulemaking, section 554(d)'s quintessentially adjudicative protections are unnecessary.

[27]   APA § 551(14) (2012).

[28]   *Id.*

[29]   Sangamon Valley v. United States, 269 F.2d 221, 224 (D.C. Cir. 1959) (holding that ex parte communications violate Due Process when the case involves "conflicting private claims to a valuable privilege.").

[30]   APA § 554(d)(1) (2012).

[31]   APA § 554(d)(2)(A)–(C) (2012).

[32]   APA § 557(d)(1) (2012).

[33]   Professional Air Traffic Controllers Org. v. FLRA, 685 F.2d 547, 570 (D.C. Cir. 1982) (holding that members of Congress and the White House are interested parties).

fact communications do not apply to ex parte *merits* communications.

If an improper ex parte communication occurs and is discovered while the action is still pending before the agency, the APA allows the agency to both cure the violation and sanction the violator. To cure the improper ex parte communication, the decision maker "shall place on the public record" all written ex parte communications and a memoranda including the substance of any oral communications.[34] Cure can be effective only if the prohibited communication is discovered before the agency reaches a final decision. In addition to curing the ex parte violation, the agency may sanction the violator by ruling against a party on the merits of a case where the party made or caused to be made a prohibited ex parte communication.[35] Note that ruling against the party must be consistent with the public interest and with the policy of the underlying agency statute.

If an improper ex parte occurs and is not discovered until after the agency renders a final decision, then the appellate court must determine whether the violation was grave enough to void the agency's decision. Courts will consider the following factors to decide whether the decision should be voided:

(1)   the gravity of the ex parte communication;

(2)   whether the ex parte communications may have influenced the agency's decision;

(3)   whether the party making the ex parte communications ultimately benefited from making them;

(4)   whether the contents of the ex parte communications were known to the other side, who would thus have had an opportunity to respond; and

(5)   whether vacating the agency's decision would serve a useful purpose.[36]

6.   *The Initial Decision*

As a result of a formal proceeding, a record is complied. The "exclusive record" includes "[t]he transcript of testimony and exhibits, together with all papers and requests filed in the proceeding."[37]

---

[34]   APA §§ 557(d)(1)(C)(i) & (ii) (2012).

[35]   APA § 557(d)(1)(D) (2012).

[36]   *Professional Air Traffic Controllers Org.*, 685 F.2d at 565 (refusing to void an agency decision despite improper ex parte communications).

[37]   APA § 556(e) (2012).

Assuming an ALJ presided at the hearing, the ALJ will make an "initial decision" after the hearing ends.[38] The ALJ must rule "on each finding, conclusion, or exception presented."[39] All decisions must include a statement of the "findings and conclusions, and the reasons or basis therefor, on all the material issues of fact, law, or discretion presented on the record; and the appropriate rule, order, sanction, relief, or denial thereof."[40] The initial decision "becomes the decision of the agency" if there is no appeal.[41]

7. Appealing the Initial Decision to the Agency

If either the regulated entity or agency[42] appeals the initial decision, then the agency head or an internal body acting for the agency head will resolve the appeal. On appeal in the agency, the agency reviews the ALJ's findings on both questions of law and fact *de novo*.[43]

If the agency's final decision is then appealed to a court, the reviewing court will evaluate the agency's factual findings to see if there is "substantial evidence" in the record to support those findings.[44] We will address this topic in Chapter 7. For now, know that the ALJ's initial decision is part of the record that the reviewing court will examine.[45] In those cases where the demeanor of the witnesses was critical to the decision, the reviewing court will consider the ALJ's demeanor findings, known as testimonial findings, because the ALJ actually observed the witnesses. Courts expect agencies to defer to the ALJ findings regarding the credibility of witnesses based on how they appeared. In contrast, agencies heads are free to reject ALJ derivative findings, findings not based on demeanor, because agencies have expertise.

Thus, although the agency head applies a *de novo* standard to review an ALJ's findings of fact, the agency should keep in mind that a reviewing court will be less likely to reverse the agency's

---

[38] APA §§ 554(d) & 557(b) (2012). if the agency prefers to retain the power to make the initial decision, it can elect to have an ALJ preside at the hearing and make a "recommended" decision. APA § 557(b).

[39] APA § 557(c)(3) (2012).

[40] APA §§ 557(c)(3)(A) & (B) (2012).

[41] APA § 557(b) (2012).

[42] Either party can appeal at this stage; however, the agency cannot appeal if the agency head rules against it. APA § 702 (providing that any "person," not including agencies, suffering legal wrong may appeal).

[43] APA § 557(b).

[44] APA § 706(2)(E).

[45] Universal Camera v. NLRB, 340 U.S. 474, 493 (1951).

final decision if it carefully considers the ALJ's findings regarding demeanor.[46]

C.   Informal Adjudication Procedures

1.   APA Procedures

The procedures above apply only to formal adjudications, not informal adjudications. Administrative judges (AJs), who lack the status and independence of the ALJs, preside over informal adjudications.

While formal adjudication resembles civil trials, informal adjudication is altogether different. Often, no hearing is offered. Indeed, few procedures are required at all; an agency need only promptly decide an issue and notify the affected party.[47] Informal adjudications can be as simple as an agency administrator approving an individual's application for a license or permit.

2.   Due Process Procedures

Although the APA requires very few procedures for informal adjudication, the U.S. Constitution or the enabling statute may require additional procedures. In cases involving the deprivation of property or liberty rights, the Due Process Clause of the U.S. Constitution requires some form of a pre-deprivation hearing.[48] Absent exigent circumstances,[49] the agency must offer some form hearing before acting, although an abbreviated form is sufficient if the agency offers a post-deprivation hearing that comports with the three *Mathews*'s requirements below.[50]

To have a constitutionally protected *property* interest, a plaintiff must show that he or she has "more than an abstract need or desire for [the interest and] more than a unilateral expectation of it."[51] The plaintiff must have a "legitimate claim of entitlement" to that interest.[52] Legitimate claims of entitlement are created and their dimensions are defined by existing rules or understandings that stem from an independent source of law, such as state law.[53]

---

[46]   *See, e.g.*, Jackson v. Veterans Admin., 786 F.2d 1322, 1330 (Fed. Cir. 1985).

[47]   APA § 552(e) (Supp. 2016).

[48]   U.S. CONST. amend. V.

[49]   *See, e.g.*, Ewing v. Mytinger & Casselberry, Inc., 339 U.S. 594, 601 (1950) (misbranded drugs); North American Cold Storage Co. v. Chicago, 211 U.S. 306, 320 (1908) (spoiled poultry).

[50]   Cleveland Bd. of Ed. v. Loudermill, 470 U.S. 532, 542 (1985).

[51]   Board of Regents v. Roth, 408 U.S. 564, 577 (1972).

[52]   *Id.*

[53]   *Id.*

To have a constitutionally protected *liberty* interest, a plaintiff must show not only that the agency will or has harmed his or her reputation but also that the plaintiff will suffer a future harm stemming from that reputational harm.[54] This test is known as "the stigma plus test." Reputational injury is the stigma; future harm is the plus. Additionally, the plaintiff must actually dispute the validity of the stigma, or there is no reason for a hearing.[55]

Assuming the plaintiff has demonstrated that an agency has or will harm a property or liberty interest, the court will determine what hearing procedures are required by balancing three competing interests identified in *Mathews*.[56] Those three interests are (1) the seriousness of the harm to the individual (the individual's interest), (2) the risk of erroneous deprivation if the requested procedures are not used (the court's interest), and (3) the administrative and fiscal burden of requiring the additional procedures (the government's interest).[57] Additionally, while an "a fair tribunal is a basic requirement of due process"[58] including a neutral decisionmaking, the fact that an agency combines investigative and adjudicative functions does not alone create an unconstitutional risk of bias because administrative officials are presumed to be honest and have integrity.[59] The plaintiff must show actual bias.

In sum, informal adjudication procedures are generally minimal, may also be governed by Due Process, and are quicker in comparison to formal adjudication procedures.

  PROCEDURES REQUIRED FOR ADJUDICATION: CHECKLIST

A. **Choice of Adjudication Procedure**—Was the agency required to use formal adjudication procedures because the enabling statute includes the phrase "on the record after a hearing" or similar words?

   1. **No**—If no, then under *Chevron*'s two-step test the agency could proceed using informal procedures. Proceed to C. below.

---

[54] Paul v. Davis, 424 U.S. 693, 702 (1976).

[55] Codd v. Velger, 429 U.S. 627 (1977).

[56] Mathews v. Eldridge, 424 U.S. 319, 335 (1976).

[57] *Id.*

[58] Withrow v. Larkin, 421 U.S. 35, 47 (1975).

[59] *Id.*

2. **Yes**—If yes, then under *Chevron*'s two-step test the agency was required to use formal procedures. To determine whether the agency correctly followed formal procedures proceed to B. below. If the agency did not use formal procedures, its choice was invalid. Stop here.

B. **Formal Adjudication Procedures**—Did the agency follow appropriate procedures?

1. Did the agency notify "persons entitled to notice of an agency hearing" regarding when and where the hearing would occur, the matters of fact alleged, the relevant law, and the agency's legal authority to hold the hearing? Was the notice sufficient to inform the regulated entity of what it did wrong?

    a. **No**—If no, then notice was insufficient and any ensuing order would be invalid under APA § 554(b). Stop here.

    b. **Yes**—If yes, then notice was sufficient to fairly apprise the interested parties of the allegations. Proceed to B.2. below.

2. Did the agency allow officials who performed investigative or prosecutorial functions supervise or oversee the ALJ who presided over the hearing?

    a. **No**—If no or if the agency head presided over the hearing, then there was no violation of the APA's separation of functions provision. Proceed to B.3. below.

    b. **Yes**—If yes, then any ensuing order would be invalid under APA § 554(d)(2). Stop here.

3. Did the proponent of the order, usually the agency, have the burden of proof?

    a. **No**—If no, then any ensuing order would be invalid under APA § 556(d). Stop here.

    b. **Yes**—If yes, then the burden was correct. Proceed to B.4. below.

4. Did the parties have the right to present their cases personally or through counsel, to present rebuttal evidence, and to conduct cross-examination *if necessary*?

    a. **No**—If no and the proceeding was not one seeking benefits, one seeking an initial license, or a formal rulemaking, then any ensuing order would be invalid.

Stop here. If the proceeding was one of the three identified, the agency may limit oral testimony and require all relevant information be submitted in writing under APA § 556(d). Proceed to B.5. below.

b. **Yes**—If yes, then proceed to B.5. below.

5. Did any communications occur that were not on the public record and to which notice to all parties was not given, other than status reports?

 a. **No**—If no, then no ex parte communications occurred as defined in APA § 551(14). Proceed to B.8. below.

 b. **Yes**—If yes, then prohibited ex parte communications may have occurred. Proceed to B.6. below to determine whether the ex parte communications were prohibited.

6. Did the ALJ (but not the agency or agency head) discuss a *fact in dispute* with anyone while not in the presence of all the parties in a proceeding other than one involving an application for an initial license or one challenging the validity or application of rates for public utilities and carriers? Note that the agency and agency head are allowed to make such communications under APA § 554(d)(2)(A)–(C).

 a. **No**—If no, then proceed to B.7. below to determine whether other communications were prohibited ex parte communications.

 b. **Yes**—If yes, then the ALJ engaged in prohibited ex parte communications under APA § 554(d)(1). To determine the remedy, ask whether the prohibited communication was discovered while the action was pending before the agency.

  i. **No**—If no, then the reviewing court will consider whether to void the order (or rule if formal rulemaking) by considering the following factors: (1) the gravity of the ex parte communications; (2) whether the ex parte communications may have influenced the agency's decision; (3) whether the party making the ex parte communications ultimately benefited from making them; (4) whether the contents of the ex parte communications were known to the other side, who would thus have had an opportunity to respond; and (5) whether vacating the agency's decision would serve a useful purpose. If the order must be voided, <u>stop here</u>. If the order is not voided for this reason, <u>proceed to B.7</u>.

     ii.   **Yes**—If yes, then the agency must cure the violation by placing the communication on the public record and must consider whether to sanction the violator under APA §§ 557(d)(1)(C)(i) & (ii). <u>Proceed to B.7</u>. to consider whether other prohibited ex parte communications took place.

   7.   Did the decision maker (the ALJ, agency, or agency head) discuss *the merits of the case* with *interested persons outside the agency* while not in the presence of all the parties?

     a.   **No**—If no, then no prohibited ex parte communications occurred. <u>Proceed to B.8. below</u>.

     b.   **Yes**—If yes, then the decision maker engaged in prohibited ex parte communications APA § 557(d)(1). To determine the remedy, ask whether the prohibited communication was discovered while the action was pending before the agency?

        i.   **No**—If no, then the reviewing court will consider whether to void the order or rule by considering the following factors: (1) the gravity of the ex parte communications; (2) whether the ex parte communications may have influenced the agency's decision; (3) whether the party making the ex parte communications ultimately benefited from making them; (4) whether the contents of the ex parte communications were known to the other side, who would thus have had an opportunity to respond; and (5) whether vacating the agency's decision would serve a useful purpose. If the order must be voided, <u>stop here</u>. If the order is not voided for this reason, <u>proceed to B.8</u>.

        ii.   **Yes**—If yes, then the agency must cure the violation by placing the communication on the public record and must consider whether to sanction the violator under APA §§ 557(d)(1)(C)(i) & (ii). <u>Proceed to B.8. below</u>.

8. On appeal to the agency, in applying *de novo* review, did the agency defer to the ALJ's testimonial findings but not the derivative findings?

    a.   **No**—If no, then a reviewing court may reverse the agency's decision as not supported by substantial evidence unless the agency had a good reason for rejecting the testimonial findings. Proceed to the checklist in Chapter 7 to determine whether the substance of the order is valid.

    b.   **Yes**—If yes, then a reviewing court is less likely to reverse the agency's findings as not supported by substantial evidence. Proceed to the checklist in Chapter 7 to determine whether the substance of order is valid.

C. **Informal Adjudication Procedures**—Did the agency follow appropriate procedures?

1. Did the agency promptly decide the issue and notify the affected party?

    a.   **No**—If no, then the agency violated the APA § 552(e) and the order is invalid. Stop here.

    b.   **Yes**—If yes, the agency complied with all procedures required by the APA, but may also have to follow additional procedures to comply with the Federal Constitution or the enabling statute. Proceed to C.2. below.

2. To determine whether Due Process applies, ask whether the regulated entity has a constitutionally protected interest.

    a.   Does the regulated entity have more than a unilateral expectation or abstract need for the interest being deprived?

        i.   **No**—If no, then the regulated entity does not have a protected property interest, but may have a protected liberty interest. Proceed to C.2.b. below.

        ii.   **Yes**—If yes, then the regulated entity has a protected property interest, and the agency must provide some form of a hearing. To determine what additional procedures are necessary, proceed to C.3. below.

    b. Will the regulated entity suffer a reputational harm and future harm as a result of the deprivation?

        i. **No**—If no, then the regulated entity does not have a protected liberty interest and, assuming the regulated entity did not have a protected property interest, has no right to any procedures other than those required by the APA. The agency's order is procedurally valid. Proceed to the checklist in Chapter 7 to determine whether the substance of the order is valid.

        ii. **Yes**—If yes, then the regulated entity has a protected liberty interest, but may not have a right to a hearing. Does the regulated entity dispute the underlying facts leading to the reputational injury?

            (a). **No**—If no, then under *Codd v. Velger*[60] the regulated entity has no right to a hearing. Stop here.

            (b). **Yes**—If yes, then the agency must provide some form of a hearing. To determine what additional procedures are necessary, proceed to C.3. below.

3. To determine what procedures apply when Due Process applies, ask the following questions.

    a. Do exigent circumstances prevent the agency from providing some form of a pre-deprivation hearing?

        i. **No**—If no, then the agency must provide some form of a pre-deprivation hearing. If the agency failed to do so, the order is invalid. Stop here. If the agency did so, proceed to C.3.b. below to determine whether the procedures provided were constitutionally sufficient.

        ii. **Yes**—If yes, then the agency may provide a post-deprivation hearing rather than a pre-deprivation hearing. Proceed to C.3.b. below to determine whether the procedures provided were constitutionally sufficient.

    b. Ask the following question for each specific procedure the regulated entity wants, such as the right to the assistance of counsel or the ability to conduct cross-

---

[60] 429 U.S. 627 (1977).

examination: Does the seriousness of the harm to the individual and the risk of erroneous deprivation if the procedure is not used outweigh the administrative and fiscal burden on the agency if it is?

i.   **No**—If no, then the agency need not provide that procedure under *Mathews v. Eldridge,*[61] and the order is procedurally valid. <u>Proceed to the checklist in Chapter 7</u> to determine whether the substance of the order is valid.

ii. **Yes**—If yes, then the agency must provide the relevant procedure and any order resulting from a hearing that did not include the procedure would be invalid. <u>Stop here</u>.

ILLUSTRATIVE PROBLEMS

■ PROBLEM 4.1 ■

Assume that the State University hired a professor to fill a "visiting professor" position. The position was for a fixed term of one academic year. At the end of the term, the professor was not re-hired. Further, the University did not provide the professor with notice that she would not be re-hired and did not provide any reason for the non-retention. Finally, the University has indicated only when asked that the professor was not rehired because the position was only needed for the one year. The professor has challenged the decision, claiming the University violated her due process rights because she was not afforded notice and an opportunity to challenge the University's decision. You are general counsel for the University and have been asked whether the professor's claim has any merit. How would you respond?

Analysis

This issue here is whether the University violated due process by not providing notice or hearing before the termination. Using the checklist above (C.2.), you should first ask whether the professor has a protected property interest in her job. Because the term of the position was fixed at one academic year, the professor had no more than a unilateral expectation in keeping her position beyond that one year; hence, she does not have a protected property interest. Moreover, because the professor will not suffer reputational harm, either in the present or future, she does not have a protected liberty

---

[61]   424 U.S. 319, 335 (1976).

interest either. Thus, the due process clause does not require the University to provide notice or a hearing.

■ **PROBLEM 4.2** ■

The Environmental Protection Agency (EPA) is involved in a formal adjudication under the APA to revoke a manufacturer's permit to market a specific pesticide because the EPA believes the pesticide is unsafe. A key *factual* issue in the adjudication is the health hazards caused by use of the pesticide. You are counsel to the EPA. You have been asked whether any of the conversations below would violate the APA?

I.   An ex parte discussion concerning the health hazards caused by use of the pesticide between the administrative law judge hearing the case and an agency scientist who is not involved in the case.

II.   An ex parte discussion concerning the health hazards caused by use of the pesticide between the administrative law judge hearing the case and a non-agency scientist, who has written widely on the subject of pesticide risk, and who is not connected to either the agency or the manufacturer.

III.   An ex parte discussion concerning the health hazards caused by use of the pesticide between the agency decision maker and an agency lawyer who is involved in prosecuting the permit revocation case. The conversation took place when the agency head was reviewing the ALJ's decision.

IV.   An ex parte discussion concerning the health hazards caused by use of the pesticide between the agency decision maker and another manufacturer of pesticides who is interested in this adjudication. The conversation took place when the agency head was reviewing the ALJ's decision.

Analysis

This issue here is whether any of the communications violate the APA's prohibitions against ex parte communications and separation of functions. Using the checklist above (B), you should first determine whether the agency officials who performed investigative or prosecutorial functions were supervised or overseen by the ALJ who presided over the hearing? The answer is no, so there was no violation of the APA's separation of functions provision. Note that the separation of functions provision does not apply to the agency decision maker, only to the ALJ.

Second, you should explain that ex parte communications occurred (according to the problem) and proceed to B.6. to determine whether the communications were prohibited. Under the APA, it is not enough that the communications are ex parte; they must also be prohibited under either APA §§ 554(d)(1) or 557(d)(1).

To determine whether any of the communications were prohibited, you should ask whether either of the communications with the ALJ were improper; these communications are in I and II above. Did the ALJ discuss a *fact in dispute* with anyone, inside or outside of the agency, while not in the presence of all parties? The answer in both cases is "yes;" the ALJ discussed the health hazards of the pesticide (a disputed issue of fact) with an agency scientist and a non-agency scientist. Thus, the ALJ engaged in prohibited ex parte communications under APA § 554(d)(1).

Next, you should ask whether any of the communications with the agency decision maker were improper; these communications are in III & IV above. The decision maker is prohibited from discussing *the merits of the case* with *interested persons outside the agency* while not in the presence of all the parties. APA § 557(d)(1). "Interested persons" includes not only the parties to the case but also anyone who has an interest in the proceeding that is greater than the interest a general member of the public would have. In III, the agency decision maker spoke to someone *inside* the agency about the merits of the case; this communication is not prohibited by the APA. In IV, however, the agency decision maker spoke to someone *outside* the agency about the health hazards of the pesticide, which relates to the merits of the case. Even though the non-party manufacturer is not a party to the case, it is likely an "interested person." As such, the ex parte communication was prohibited by APA § 557(d)(1).

Finally, to determine the remedy for the violations above, you should ask whether the prohibited communication was discovered while the action was pending before the agency. If yes, then the agency must cure the violation by placing the communication on the public record and must consider whether to sanction the violator under APA §§ 557(d)(1)(C)(i) & (ii). If no, then the reviewing court will consider whether to void the order (or rule if formal rulemaking) by considering the following factors: (1) the gravity of the ex parte communications; (2) whether the ex parte communications may have influenced the agency's decision; (3) whether the party making the ex parte communications ultimately benefited from making them; (4) whether the contents of the ex parte communications were known to the other side, who would thus have had an opportunity to respond; and (5) whether vacating the agency's decision would serve a useful purpose.

POINTS TO REMEMBER

- A court will evaluate an agency's decision to use informal procedures using the *Chevron* two-step test. Under this standard, unless the language of the statute is very clear that Congress wanted the agency to use formal procedures (includes "on the record after an opportunity for an agency hearing"), an agency's decision to use informal procedures will likely be upheld as reasonable.

- The same procedures apply both to formal rulemaking and formal adjudication; however, formal rulemaking is less common.

- When an agency conducts formal adjudication or rulemaking, it must essentially provide a trial-like hearing, with notice, the right to counsel, and the ability to cross-examine witnesses. However, the rules of evidence do not apply.

- Pursuant to the separation of functions prohibition in the APA, an investigator or prosecutor cannot supervise an ALJ.

- There are two ex parte prohibitions in the APA: First, an ALJ cannot discuss *facts is dispute* in a case with *anyone* inside or outside the agency, except in the presence of all other parties. Second, any agency decision maker cannot discuss *the merits of the case* with *interested persons outside* the agency.

- If prohibited ex parte communications occur, the agency must cure and may sanction the violating party.

- Courts may void any agency action if improper ex parte occurred and was not cured at the agency level.

CHAPTER 5

What Procedures Are Required for Investigation & Disclosure?

In the last two chapters, you learned the procedures the APA requires an agency to follow when it engages in rulemaking and adjudication. This chapter addresses the procedures an agency must follow when it wishes to obtain information either through an investigation or disclosure. As with rulemaking and adjudication, the agency acts pursuant to the applicable procedures provided in the APA and the Constitution. Additionally, however, agencies must follow a number of other statutes when it discloses information to the public or holds meetings.

REVIEW

It is unlikely that your professor will test you on this subject matter. It is often the last subject covered in Administrative Law courses, if it is covered at all. However, this chapter addresses a large part of what agencies do; hence, a law professor's oversight of this important area may seem odd to a practitioner. In case you are tested on this information or encounter an issue in practice, here is what you need to know.

A. Agency Power to Investigate

Agencies obtain information from citizens and businesses in two ways. First, an agency may require that citizens produce information in documentary or testimonial form, either "voluntarily" through reports (such as your annual income tax return) or by compulsion in the form of a subpoena. Second, an agency may conduct a physical inspection of a residence or place of business to gather information relevant to some regulatory or enforcement standard. Again, compliance may be voluntary or forced through a warrant.

1. Documents and Testimony

The primary way agencies collect information is by obtaining documents (records and reports). Regulated entities may be required by statute or subpoena to provide written reports or to complete forms. Because agencies' demand for such information has mushroomed in recent years, Congress has required agencies to maintain minimal standards of necessity, efficiency, non-duplication, and interagency coordination.[1]

a. Voluntary Production

Most individuals and businesses willingly provide information to the government either because they feel obligated to do so or because they want something in return, for example a tax refund, a license to practice law, financial aid, or a global entry pass. Additionally, the government can compel disclosure by issuing a subpoena.

b. Involuntary Production

Agencies can compel regulated entities to provide information by way of a subpoena or a subpoena *duces tecum*. A subpoena seeks testimony, while a subpoena *duces tecum* seeks documents. Federal agencies do not have the power to enforce a subpoena. If someone refuses to comply, the agency must go to federal court to obtain an order of compliance.

A court will "quash," or refuse to enforce, a subpoena in three situations. First, a court will quash a subpoena if the agency does not have statutory authority to issue the subpoena; it is rare for an agency to not have such authority.

Second, a court will quash a subpoena if it violates the Fourth Amendment of the Federal Constitution. This Amendment protects "[t]he right of the people to be secure in their persons, houses, papers, and effects, against unreasonable searches and seizures."[2] To prevail on its action to enforce a subpoena, an agency must prove that (1) the subpoena was issued for a congressionally authorized purpose, (2) the information sought is relevant to an authorized purpose, and (3) the information sought is adequately described.[3] Because courts interpret these elements liberally, the Fourth

---

[1]   *See, e.g.*, Paperwork Reduction Act, 44 U.S.C. § 3501 (2012); Information Quality Act, 44 U.S.C. § 3516 (2012).

[2]   U.S. CONST. amend IV.

[3]   United States v. Sturm, Ruger Co., Inc., 84 F.3d 1, 4 (1st Cir. 1996).

Amendment provides little protection to those trying to quash a subpoena.

Third, a court will quash a subpoena if it violates the Fifth Amendment of the Federal Constitution. This Amendment protects people from "be[ing] compelled in any criminal case to be a witness against himself."[4] While administrative agencies are not normally engaged in criminal law enforcement, administrative action may lead to criminal prosecution. Generally, the scope of the Fifth Amendment is explored in Constitutional Law and Criminal Procedure courses, not Administrative Law courses.

For our purposes, here is the law in a nutshell: the Supreme Court has interpreted the Fifth Amendment principally to restrict the government's power to compel natural persons to testify orally against themselves if testifying would lead to criminal prosecution. With one very limited exception,[5] the Fifth Amendment does not apply to the production of records that were voluntarily[6] or involuntarily created.[7] To be clear, the Fifth Amendment does not protect artificial entities from producing incriminating business records; it does not protect the custodian of business records from producing incriminating records, even when the custodian would be implicated personally by the production; it does not protect the owners of sole proprietorships from producing involuntarily created public records; and it does not protect the owners of sole proprietorships from producing voluntarily created documents unless the act of production itself would be incriminating.

2.   *Inspections*

a.   Voluntary Compliance

Most individuals and businesses willingly comply with inspection requests, because non-compliance has costs, including negative publicity and a lack of good will in the future from the agency both short and long term.

---

[4]   U.S. CONST., amend. V.

[5]   The act of production exception provides that while the contents of a document may not be privileged because it was voluntarily created, the very act of producing the document may be privileged if would serve as testimony that a crime occurred. United States v. Hubbell, 530 U.S. 27, 36–37 (2000); Braswell v. United States, 487 U.S. 99, 117–18 (1988).

[6]   Fisher v. United States, 425 U.S. 391, 407–09 (1976).

[7]   Shapiro v. United States, 335 U.S. 1, 34 (1948) (holding that various records a wholesaler of fruit and produce was obliged to keep under the Emergency Price Control Act were not protected from disclosure by the Fifth Amendment).

b.Involuntary Compliance

If the regulated entity refuses to allow an inspection, the agency may go to court to obtain a search warrant. To comply with the Fourth Amendment, the agency seeking the search warrant must demonstrate *administrative probable cause,* meaning either that the agency has specific evidence that the regulated entity is violating the law or that a statute or regulation allows periodic inspections and this inspection falls within the statutory or regulatory parameters.[8]

Importantly, a warrant is not required for every search. There are several well-recognized exceptions to the warrant requirement, including (1) searches of locations in plain view,[9] (2) searches in emergency situations,[10] (3) searches subject to informed consent,[11] and (4) searches of "closely," or "pervasively," regulated businesses.[12] The closely regulated business exception to the warrant requirement is essentially an outgrowth of the implied consent doctrine: by voluntarily engaging in a heavily regulated business, business owners give up their expectations of privacy. To date, the following businesses have been found to be closely regulated: liquor dealers;[13] weapon dealers;[14] stone quarries;[15] and junkyards engaging in vehicle dismantling.[16]

---

[8]*See* Marshall v. Barlow's, Inc., 436 U.S. 307, 320 (1978) (explaining that the "[p]robable cause justifying the issuance of a warrant [in the administrative context] may be based not only on specific evidence of an existing violation but also on a showing that reasonable legislative or administrative standards for conducting an . . . inspection are satisfied.").

[9]*See, e.g.,* Air Pollution Variance Bd. v. Western Alfalfa Corp., 416 U.S. 861, 864–65 (1974) (upholding an inspection of factory emissions from smokestacks when those emissions were visible from outside the factory).

[10]*See, e.g.,* North Am. Cold Storage Co. v. Chicago, 211 U.S. 306 (1908) (allowing seizure of unwholesome food); Jacobson v. Massachusetts, 197 U.S. 11, 37 (1905) (allowing compulsory smallpox vaccination); Campagnie Francaise De Navigation A Vapeur v. Louisiana State Bd. of Health, 186 U.S. 380, 397 (1902) (allowing health quarantine).

[11]*See, e.g.,* Vernonia School District 47J v. Acton, 515 U.S. 646, 664–65 (1995) (holding that public school student athletes could be subject to urinalysis testing because they elected to participate in school activities); Board of Ed. v. Earls, 536 U.S. 822, 837–38 (2002) (extending *Vernonia School District*'s holding to all public school students who wished to participate in after school activities); *but see* Safford Unified School District #1 v. Redding, 557 U.S. 364, 376 (2009) (holding that that the strip search of a thirteen-year-old girl by public school officials who were searching for drugs violated the Fourth Amendment).

[12]Colonnade Catering Corp. v. United States, 397 U.S. 72, 77 (1970) (allowing warrantless search of liquor licensee); United States v. Biswell, 406 U.S. 311, 315 (1972) (allowing warrantless search of gun dealer).

[13]*Colonnade Catering Corp.,* 397 U.S. at 77.

[14]*Biswell,* 406 U.S. at 315.

[15]Donovan v. Dewey, 452 U.S. 594, 602–03 (1981).

[16]New York v. Burger, 482 U.S. 691, 707 (1987).

Because administrative proceedings are civil in nature, the exclusionary rule generally does not apply.[17] However, in some cases in which a civil penalty was involved, lower courts have applied the exclusionary rule.[18]

B. Agency Duty to Disclose

1. The Freedom of Information Act

If your professor decides to test information in this chapter, it is likely this topic will be addressed. The Freedom of Information Act (FOIA)[19] is critically important to both agencies and the public.

FOIA requires that agencies provide information to the public in three ways. First, FOIA requires that agencies publish certain information in the Federal Register.[20] Such information includes agency descriptions, addresses, rules of procedure, and forms for all reports and examinations. Further, agencies must publish "substantive rules of general applicability . . . and statements of general policy or interpretations."[21] In other words, agencies must publish non-legislative rules in the Federal Register.

Second, FOIA requires that agencies make certain information available for inspection and copying, including all final opinions and orders in adjudicated cases.[22] Full indexing is required for ease of access. And FOIA provides that matters not properly published or indexed are not binding on a regulated entity unless the regulated entity had actual notice of them.[23]

Third, the best known, and most likely tested, requirement in FOIA is that agencies must make some records available upon request. FOIA provides: "[E]ach agency, upon request for records which . . . reasonably describe such records . . . shall make such records promptly available to any person."[24] FOIA's definition of "agency" is broader than the definition in APA § 551(1). FOIA's definition includes both executive branch and independent agencies, government-owned and government-controlled

---

[17] United States v. Janis, 428 U.S. 433, 459–60 (1976); *see* INS v. Lopez-Mendoza, 468 U.S. 1032, 1033 (1984); Pennsylvania Bd. of Probation & Parole v. Scott, 524 U.S. 357, 363 (1998).

[18] *See, e.g.,* Trinity Industries, Inc. v. OSHRC, 16 F.3d 1455, 1461–62 (6th Cir. 1994); Lakeland Enters. of Rhinelander, Inc. v. Chao, 402 F.3d 739, 744–45 (7th Cir. 2005).

[19] FOIA is part of the APA and is codified in section 552.

[20] APA § 552(a)(1) (Supp. 2016).

[21] APA § 552(a)(1)(D) (Supp. 2016).

[22] APA § 552(a)(2) (Supp. 2016).

[23] *Id.*

[24] APA § 552(a)(3)(A) (Supp. 2016).

corporations, and the executive office; however, FOIA does not apply to the president, the president's personal staff, and entities that exist solely to advise the president.[25] Further, FOIA does not apply to Congress or the federal courts.

"Any person" may make a FOIA request, including any "individual, partnership, corporation, association, or public or private organization other than an agency."[26] Subject to only a couple of narrow exceptions, the purpose of the requester is not relevant to the agency's obligation to disclose.[27] A requester need only "reasonably describe the record."[28] Then, the agency must make a good faith search of its files for the requested record.[29] In some situations, agencies may impose reasonable charges for their costs in searching for and copying records.[30] For example, agencies may charge reasonable fees for document search, duplication, and review, when records are requested for commercial use.[31]

Not all information must be disclosed. FOIA contains nine types of information that are exempted from disclosure: (1) classified information; (2) internal agency personnel rules and practices; (3) matters that another statute specifically exempts from disclosure; (4) trade secrets and commercial or financial information that the agency obtained from someone other than the requester; (5) inter-agency or intra-agency memoranda and letters, not otherwise available through discovery in a civil action against the agency; (6) personnel files, medical files, and similar files, the disclosure of which would constitute a clearly unwarranted invasion of personal privacy; (7) records and information compiled for law enforcement purposes; (8) matters related to the regulation of banks and other financial institutions; and (9) geological and geophysical information.[32] Notably, a regulated entity that wants to prevent an agency from disclosing material the regulated entity believes should

---

[25] *See* Kissinger v. Reporters Comm. for Freedom of the Press, 445 U.S. 136, 156 (1980) (holding that FOIA did not apply to the National Security Council and the Council of Economic Advisors).

[26] APA § 551(2) (2012). The phrase includes foreign governments and aliens, although since 9/11, Congress has placed some limits on the ability of foreign governments to obtain records. APA § 552(a)(3)(E)(i) (Supp. 2016).

[27] *See, e.g.*, Durns v. Bureau of Prisons, 804 F.2d 701, 706 (D.C. Cir. 1986) (saying, "Congress granted the scholar and the scoundrel equal rights of access to federal records under the FOIA.").

[28] APA § 552(a)(3)(A).

[29] *See* APA §§ 552(a)(3)(C) & (D) (Supp. 2016).

[30] APA § 552(a)(4)(A)(ii) (Supp. 2016).

[31] APA § 552(a)(4)(A)(ii)(I) (Supp. 2016).

[32] APA § 552(b)(1)–(9) (Supp. 2016).

be exempt cannot sue to prevent the disclosure. Such reverse FOIA claims are not allowed.[33]

When a request for documents is made to an agency, the agency has twenty days to determine whether one of the above exceptions applies and to notify the requester whether the agency plans to comply with the request.[34] If the agency denies the request in part or whole, the agency must provide an explanation and information about how to appeal its decision internally.[35] Internal agency appeals are subject to a similarly short time frame. After any internal appeal, and assuming the agency denied the internal appeal, the requester may seek judicial review immediately in a federal district court.[36]

On appeal, the court will decide *de novo* whether the agency's decision to withhold the information was valid.[37] It is the agency's burden to prove that its failure to disclose was legal.[38] Moreover, the court may award a requester who "substantially prevails" attorneys' fees and costs.[39]

Despite these tight deadlines, agencies often do not respond promptly. Agencies heavy workload has frustrated Congress's clear desire for "prompt" agency response. No one anticipated the tremendous volume of requests FOIA would generate. And courts have been understandably sympathetic to the agencies' cries of request overload.

2. *The Government in Sunshine Act*

Congress enacted the Government in the Sunshine Act, or the Sunshine Act, in 1976, during a time when Congress believed that government functions should be open to public inspection.[40] The Sunshine Act requires that "every portion of every meeting of an agency . . . be open to public observation."[41] It provides further that agencies must provide advance notice of meetings to ensure the public is aware of them.[42] Note that the public has no right to participate, only to observe.

---

[33] Chrysler v. Brown, 441 U.S. 281, 285 (1979).

[34] APA § 552(a)(6) (Supp. 2016); APA § 552(a)(6)(A)(i) (Supp. 2016).

[35] APA § 552(a)(6).

[36] APA § 552(a)(4)(B) (Supp. 2016).

[37] *Id.*

[38] *Id.*

[39] APA § 552(a)(E) (Supp. 2016).

[40] Pub. L. 94–409, 90 Stat. 1241, enacted September 13, 1976, 5 U.S.C. § 552b. It is codified directly after FOIA at APA § 552b.

[41] APA § 552b(b) (2012).

[42] APA § 552b(b)(e) (2012).

Although the language quoted above appears broad, the Sunshine Act narrowly defines both "agency" and "meeting." First, the Sunshine Act defines "agency" as one "headed by a collegial body composed of two or more individual members, a majority of whom are appointed to such position by the President and with the advice of the Senate."[43] Thus, the Sunshine Act applies only to the so-called independent agencies, such as the Federal Communications Commission, the Securities and Exchange Commission, and the Federal Trade Commission, because multi-member bodies typically head independent agencies. In contrast, individuals typically head executive agencies. Because these agency heads have no one with whom to deliberate, their deliberations need not be public.

Second, the Sunshine Act defines "meeting" as "the deliberations of at least the number of individual agency members required to take action on behalf of the agency where such deliberations determine or result in the joint conduct or disposition of official agency business."[44] There is no requirement that the members meet in person; a telephone or video call counts. The definition of "meeting" includes three requirements for a gathering of agency members to be covered: (1) the number of agency members must constitute a quorum of the agency or a subpart that has power to act on behalf of the agency; (2) the agency members must deliberate, but not necessarily decide anything;[45] and (3) the deliberations must "determine or result in the joint conduct or disposition of official agency business."[46]

Like FOIA, the Sunshine Act allows an agency to hold a closed meeting when the discussion involves one of ten exempt matters and when the public interest does not require otherwise. Seven of those ten track FOIA's exemptions,[47] while three are unique to the

---

[43]   APA § 552b(b).

[44]   APA § 552b(a)(2) (2012).

[45]   *See, e.g.,* FCC v. ITT World Commc'ns, Inc., 466 U.S. 463, 471 (1984) (stating that the Sunshine Act applies if the discussions are "sufficiently focused . . . as to cause or be likely to cause the individual participating members to form reasonably firm positions regarding matters pending or likely to arise before the agency.").

[46]   APA § 552b(a)(2).

[47]   APA § 552b(c)(1)–(4) & (6)–(8) (2012), which provide as follows:

(1) disclose matters that are . . . to be kept secret in the interests of national defense or foreign policy. . .;

(2) relate solely to the internal personnel rules and practices of an agency;

(3) disclose matters specifically exempted from disclosure by [another] statute;

(4) disclose trade secrets and commercial or financial information obtained from a person and privileged or confidential;

Sunshine Act. The unique ones allow for closed meeting when the meeting "[1] involve[s] accusing any person of a crime, or formally censuring any person; [2] [involves] disclos[ing] information the premature disclosure of which would . . . be likely to significantly frustrate implementation of a proposed agency action . . .; or [3] specifically concern[s] the agency's issuance of a subpoena, or the agency's participation in a civil action or proceeding . . . ."[48]

Judicial enforcement of the Sunshine Act is similar to judicial enforcement of FOIA. "Any person" can bring suit in federal district court against an agency that violates the Act.[49] The agency carries the burden to prove that its decision not to open its meeting was legal.[50] Attorney fees and costs are also available.[51]

Importantly, a court cannot invalidate an agency action solely on the ground that the agency failed to abide by the Sunshine Act.[52] Thus, a litigant should sue before the meeting; otherwise, the litigant's only remedy may be to obtain a transcript of the illegally closed meeting.[53]

3. The Federal Advisory Committee Act

The Federal Advisory Committee Act (FACA)[54] applies to federal advisory committees, which are composed of private individuals and are established to help Congress and the executive branch make law and policy and award grants. These committees have offered advice on various topics from organ transplant practices to improving operations at the Department of Homeland Security. FACA enhances public scrutiny of and participation in advisory committees in several ways. Specifically, meetings must be announced in advance and be open to the public.[55] "Interested persons" must be given a chance "to attend, appear before, or file statements with any advisory committee."[56] Relevant documents

---

(6) disclose information of a personal nature where disclosure would constitute a clearly unwarranted invasion of personal privacy;

(7) disclose investigatory records compiled for law enforcement purposes . . .;

(8) disclose information contained in or related to . . . financial institutions.

[48]   APA § 552b(c)(5) & (9)–(10) (2012).

[49]   APA § 552b(h) (2012).

[50]   *Id.*

[51]   APA § 552b(j) (2012).

[52]   *See* APA § 552b(h)(2) (2012).

[53]   *Cf.* Common Cause v. NRC, 674 F.2d 921, 923 (D.C. Cir. 1982).

[54]   *See* Pub. L. 92–463, § 1, Oct. 6, 1972, 86 Stat. 770. It can be found at 5 U.S.C. App. 2. [hereinafter FACA].

[55]   FACA §§ 10(a)(1) & (2) (2012).

[56]   FACA § 10(a)(3) (2012).

and minutes must be publicly available.[57] Also, the exemptions that apply under the Sunshine Act and FOIA also apply.[58]

FACA defines a federal advisory committee broadly as "any committee, board, commission, council, conference, panel, task force, or other similar group, or any subcommittee . . . established by statute or reorganization plan, . . . established or utilized by the President, or . . . established or utilized by one or more agencies" to obtain advice or recommendations.[59]

Unlike the other open-government laws, which exempt the president, FACA expressly applies to the president. But the Supreme Court has, in the past, expressed separation of powers concerns when Congress has interfered with the president's constitutionally assigned functions.[60]

Finally, unlike FOIA and the Sunshine Act, FACA does not provide for judicial review.[61]

          PROCEDURES REQUIRED FOR
INVESTIGATION: CHECKLIST

A. **Information Gathering**—Did the agency seek information or disclose information?

    1. **No**—If no, then <u>return to the checklist in Chapter 1</u>. You have made a mistake in identifying the type of agency action at issue.

    2. **Yes**—If yes, then <u>proceed to B.1. below if the agency sought information and to C.1. below if the agency disclosed information</u>.

B. **Information Flowing to the Agency**—

    1. Did the agency seek information in documentary or testimonial form?

        a. **No**—If no, <u>proceed to B.2. below</u>.

---

[57] FACA §§ 10(b) & (c) (2012).

[58] FACA §§ 10(b) & (d) (2012).

[59] FACA § 3(2) (2012).

[60] *See, e.g.*, Public Citizen v. DOJ, 491 U.S. 440, 455 (1989) (holding that the American Bar Association's Standing Committee on the Federal Judiciary was not an advisory committee under FACA).

[61] However, the courts have allowed plaintiffs who were personally injured to file an action for violations of some of the act's provisions. *See, e.g.*, Alabama-Tombigbee Rivers Coalition v. DOI, 26 F.3d 1103, 1107 (11th Cir. 1994) (finding injunctive relief an appropriate remedy when an agency failed to satisfy the requirements for committee meetings proscribed in FACA).

b. **Yes**—If yes, proceed to B.1.c. below.

c. **Voluntary Nature of the Production**—Did the regulated entity voluntarily provide the information?

    i. **No**—If no, proceed to B.1.d. below.

    ii. **Yes**—If yes, then stop here. The agency can ask for information and the regulated entity can voluntarily provide that information.

d. **Involuntary Production**—Did the agency go to court to compel compliance with an agency subpoena (for testimony) or subpoena *duces tecum* (for documents)?

    i. **No**—If no, stop here. The agency has no independent power to enforce its subpoena and must go to federal court.

    ii. **Yes**—If yes, then proceed to B.1.e. below.

e. **Motion to Quash Subpoena**—

    i. Did the agency prove that it has statutory authority to issue the subpoena?

        (a). No—If no, stop here. The court should quash the subpoena because the agency does not have statutory authority to issue the subpoena.

        (b). Yes—If yes, proceed to B.1.e.ii. below.

    ii. Did the agency prove that (1) the subpoena was issued for a congressionally authorized purpose, (2) the information sought was relevant to an authorized purpose, and (3) the information sought was adequately described?

        (a). No—If no, stop here. The court should quash the subpoena because it violates the Fourth Amendment of the Constitution.

        (b). Yes—If yes, proceed to B.1.e.iii. below.

    iii. Did the person moving to quash the subpoena prove that it would compel an individual, not a business, to testify *orally* against himself and that testifying would lead to criminal prosecution?

        (a). No—If no, proceed to B.1.e.iv. below.

          (b). Yes—If yes, <u>stop here</u>. The court should quash the subpoena because it violates the Fifth Amendment of the Constitution.

    iv. Did the person moving to quash the subpoena prove that it would compel an individual, not a business, to produce voluntarily created documents, not involuntarily created documents, and that the very act of production could serve as proof that a crime occurred?

          (a). No—If no, then the court should not quash the subpoena, and the regulated entity must comply. <u>Stop here.</u>

          (b). Yes—If yes, <u>stop here</u>. The court should quash the subpoena because it violates the Fifth Amendment of the Constitution. But this is likely the wrong answer because the act of production doctrine is so narrow you have likely missed one of the elements.

2. Did the agency seek to inspect a regulated entity?

    a. **No**—If no, you have made a mistake. <u>Return to A.1.</u>

    b. **Yes**—If yes, <u>proceed to B.2.c. below</u>.

    c. **Voluntary Nature of the Production**—Did the regulated entity voluntarily allow the inspection?

        i. **No**—If no, <u>proceed to B.2.d. below</u>.

        ii. **Yes**—If yes, then <u>stop here</u>. The agency can ask for to inspect and the regulated entity can voluntarily allow the inspection.

    d. **Involuntary Production**—Does the agency need a warrant to conduct the inspection?

        i. Is the location to be searched in plain view?

          (a). No—If no, <u>proceed to B.2.d.ii. below</u>.

          (b). Yes—If yes, then <u>stop here</u>. A warrant is not needed under the Fourth Amendment. The search is valid.

        ii. Is there an emergency that justifies a search?

          (a). No—If no, <u>proceed to B.2.d.iii. below</u>.

          (b). Yes—If yes, then <u>stop here</u>. A warrant is not needed under the Fourth Amendment. The search is valid.

   iii. Is the search conducted pursuant to informed consent?

    (a). No—If no, <u>proceed to B.2.d.iv. below</u>.

    (b). Yes—If yes, then <u>stop here</u>. A warrant is not needed under the Fourth Amendment. The search is valid.

   iv. Is the search of a closely regulated business, such as a liquor dealer, weapon dealer, stone quarries, or dismantling junkyard?

    (a). No—If no, then <u>stop here</u>. A warrant is required. However, the agency need only show administrative probable cause, meaning the statute or regulation allows periodic inspections and this inspection falls within the statutory parameters.

    (b). Yes—If yes, then <u>stop here</u>. A warrant is not needed under the Fourth Amendment. The search is valid.

C. Information Flowing from the Agency—

 1. Did a requester seek information from the agency?

  a. **No**—If no, <u>proceed to C.2. below</u>. FOIA does not apply.

  b. **Yes**—If yes, <u>proceed to C.1.c. below</u>.

  c. Does one of the nine exceptions in APA § 552(b)(1)–(9) apply?

   i. **No**—If no, <u>stop here</u>. FOIA applies, and the information must be disclosed. The requester can sue in federal court; if the requester substantially prevails, the court may award costs and attorneys' fees.

  b. **Yes**—If yes, <u>stop here</u>. The agency is allowed to withhold the information.

 2. Did the agency hold a meeting with a quorum of its members, to deliberate, which resulted in the disposition of official agency business that was not open to the public?

  a. **No**—If no, <u>proceed to C.3. below</u>. The Sunshine Act does not apply, and the meeting did not need to be open to the public.

  b. **Yes**—If yes, <u>proceed to C.2.c. below</u>.

    c. Does one of the ten exceptions in APA § 552b(c)(1)–(10) apply?

        i. **No**—If no, <u>stop here</u>. The Sunshine Act applies, and the meeting should have been open to the public. If the meeting has not yet occurred, anyone can sue to have the meeting opened. If the meeting already occurred, the only judicial remedy is likely to be a transcript of the illegally closed meeting, costs, and attorneys' fees.

        ii. **Yes**—If yes, <u>stop here</u>. The agency is allowed to conduct a closed meeting.

  3. Did the agency hold a meeting with "any committee, board, commission, council, conference, panel, task force, or other similar group, or any subcommittee . . . established by statute or reorganization plan, . . . established or utilized by the President, or . . . established or utilized by one or more agencies" that was not open to the public?

    a. **No**—If no, <u>stop here</u>. FACA does not apply, and the meeting did not need to be open to the public.

    b. **Yes**—If yes, <u>proceed to C.3.c. below</u>.

    c. Does one of the exceptions in FACA §§ 10(b) & (d) apply?

        i. **No**—If no, <u>stop here</u>. FACA applies, and the meeting should have been open to the public. However, FACA does not provide for judicial review.

        ii. **Yes**—If yes, <u>stop here</u>. The agency is allowed to conduct a closed meeting.

ILLUSTRATIVE PROBLEMS

■ PROBLEM 5.1 ■

Assume that you represent the owner of a junk yard that dismantles vehicles. An agency inspector has appeared at your client's door asking for permission to inspect the premises. Assuming your client does not wish to agree to the inspection, may the inspector inspect the plant without a warrant?

Analysis

This issue here is whether the agency must first obtain a warrant before conducting an involuntary inspection. Using the checklist above (2.d.), you should ask whether any of the exceptions apply: plain view, emergency, informed consent, or closely regulated business.

Here, the problem notes that the client operates a dismantling junkyard, which is a closely regulated business. According to *New York v. Burger*, 482 U.S. 691, 702–03 (1987), the Fourth Amendment applies, but it does not require either a warrant or probable cause. Rather the standard for a valid warrantless search is threefold: (1) the regulatory scheme has to be justified by a substantial governmental interest, (2) warrantless inspections must be necessary to further the regulatory scheme, and (3) the terms of the inspection must provide a constitutionally adequate substitute for a warrant. This third requirement requires that the scheme be detailed enough to put regulated entities on notice that they are subject to periodic inspections and that the scheme limit the inspector's discretion, requiring the inspector to act reasonably.

■ PROBLEM 5.2 ■

Assume that you are a staff attorney for the Occupational Safety and Health Administration (OSHA). The enabling statute specifically authorizes OSHA to conduct inspections "when it receives a complaint that a workplace safety violation exists." According to the statute, "the purpose of any inspection is for the agency to determine whether a violation of safety laws occurred." An employee of Manufacturer, Inc. complained to OSHA that Manufacturer, Inc. was violating specific safety regulations; the violations do not present an emergency that needs immediate attention. Manufacturer, Inc. is not a liquor dealer, weapons' dealer, stone quarry, or dismantling junkyard. The OSHA Administrator asks you whether it must obtain a warrant prior to inspecting Manufacturer, Inc. and whether the inspection may be comprehensive (a wall-to-wall search) or must be limited to the allegations in the employee's complaint. How do you respond?

Analysis

This issue here is whether OSHA must obtain a search warrant and, if so, what the limits are on the search. Using the checklist above (B.1.), you should note that the agency is not seeking information in either documentary or testimonial form and proceed to B.2. Pursuant to B.2., OSHA is seeking to inspect a regulated entity. Assuming that Manufacturer's, Inc. is not willing to allow the inspection voluntarily, then a warrant is needed unless an exception applies. No exception seems to apply: (1) the locations to be searched do not appear to be within plain view; (2) the violations do not rise to the level of an emergency; (3) the search would not be conducted pursuant to informed consent; (4) the search is not of a closely regulated business. Absent an exception to the warrant requirement, agencies must obtain a warrant prior to a search, even when a statute provides authority to the agency to search. Hence, a warrant is necessary in this case.

Under the terms of the enabling statute, the employee complaints would serve as administrative probable cause for a warrant to issue. The ensuing inspection must be within the statutory parameters. In this case, the statute grants OSHA authority to conduct an inspection that is limited to "determin[ing] whether a violation of safety laws occurred" when OSHA receives a complaint. OSHA cannot conduct a "wall-to-wall" search.

POINTS TO REMEMBER

- Citizens and business overwhelmingly provide information to agencies voluntarily.

- Agencies must have a statutory grant of authority to request information if a regulated entity is unwilling to provide the information voluntarily.

- Pursuant to the Fourth Amendment, an agency can subpoena records if it has statutory authority, the records are relevant, and the request is not oppressively broad.

- If necessary, agencies must seek to enforce their subpoenas in court.

- Regarding oral *testimony*, the Fifth Amendment protects individuals from being compelled to testify against themselves.

- Regarding the production of *documents*, the Fifth Amendment provides very little protection.

- Most regulated entities voluntarily comply with inspection requests.

- Agencies must have a statutory grant of authority to conduct an inspection.

- Pursuant to the Fourth Amendment, an agency needs a warrant to conduct an inspection; however, the agency need only show that the inspection complies with "reasonable legislative or administrative standards."

- Agencies do not need a warrant to inspect closely regulated businesses.

- The Freedom of Information Act requires that agencies provide information to the public (1) by publishing certain information in the Federal Register, (2) by making certain information available for inspection and copying, and (3) by responding to requestor's requests.

- FOIA contains nine types of information that are exempt from disclosure.

- The Government in the Sunshine Act requires that meetings involving the deliberations of independent agencies must be open to the public, subject to ten exemptions.

- The Federal Advisory Committee Act enhances public involvement in advisory committees and their meetings but is not judicially enforceable.

CHAPTER 6

Is Judicial Review of the Agency's Action Available?

I n Chapter 1, you learned to identify the type of agency action. In Chapter 2, you learned to evaluate whether the agency had statutory and constitutional power to act. In Chapters 3, 4, and 5, you learned what procedures the APA requires for the various types of actions an agency can take. In the next two chapters, we look at what happens when an agency acts and someone or something is unhappy with that action. In this chapter, you will learn about the doctrines limiting the unhappy person's ability to obtain judicial review of the agency's action. In Chapter 7, you will learn what standard of review a court will apply, assuming the unhappy person is able to get into court.

REVIEW

This chapter addresses the *availability* of judicial review. To determine whether judicial review is available, you must determine the answer to three questions. First, you must determine whether the court can hear the specific claim, meaning the plaintiff must demonstrate that the court has jurisdiction and that the plaintiff has a cause of action. Second, you must determine whether this particular plaintiff can sue, meaning the plaintiff can demonstrate that he or she has constitutional, prudential, and statutory standing. Third, you must determine whether the plaintiff can sue now or must wait for something further to occur, meaning the plaintiff must demonstrate finality, exhaustion, and ripeness. All of these doctrines are explained below.

A.   The Court & the Claim

1.   Jurisdiction

The first question in every case filed in federal court is whether that court has jurisdiction to hear the particular claim. Jurisdiction focuses on the courts' power to hear the claim itself. This power must come from a statute other than the APA, because the APA contains no jurisdiction-granting language.

Often, Congress explicitly grants jurisdiction to federal courts in the agency's enabling statute. However, even when Congress fails to grant jurisdiction in the enabling statute, the general federal question statute provides federal courts with jurisdiction to hear "all civil actions arising under the Constitution, law, or treaties of the United States."[1] Hence, jurisdiction over a claim against an agency is rarely a problem.

2.   Cause of Action

In addition to establishing that the court has jurisdiction, a plaintiff must demonstrate that he or she has a cause of action, meaning that some statute grants this particular plaintiff a right to sue. When Congress provides a jurisdictional grant of jurisdiction in an enabling statute, Congress also typically provides the plaintiff with a cause of action. For example, an enabling statute might provide that any person who is adversely affected by the agency's action may file a petition challenging the validity of that action in federal court.[2] Judicial review pursuant to a specific grant like this one is called statutory review and comes with its own procedural requirements. We will not focus on those specific requirements, because they will vary with each enabling statute.

For those agency actions where Congress has not provided for judicial review in the statute (a fact pattern you are more likely to see on an Administrative Law exam), the APA provides that any "person suffering legal wrong because of agency action, or adversely affected or aggrieved by agency action within the meaning of a relevant statute, is entitled to judicial review thereof."[3] Judicial review pursuant to the APA is often called "non-statutory review," even though the APA is a statute. We will focus on the three APA requirements for non-statutory review next.

---

[1]   28 U.S.C. § 1331 (2012).
[2]   *See, e.g.*, 29 U.S.C. § 655(f) (2012).
[3]   APA § 702 (2012).

a. Agency Action

First, for a plaintiff to have a cause of action, the court must find that what the agency did was agency action. The APA defines "agency action" as "includ[ing] the whole or a part of an agency rule, order, license, sanction, relief, or the equivalent or denial thereof, or failure to act."[4] Generally, a plaintiff can easily meet this requirement, because this definition is so broad.

So let's take a look at two cases in which the plaintiffs were unable to demonstrate that the challenged decision was agency action. First, the Supreme Court held that the Bureau of Land Management's (BLM) decision to reclassify public lands for mining individually rather than collectively was not agency action subject to judicial review.[5] While each individual BLM decision regarding a specific piece of land would be agency action, the Court held that the BLM's decision to consider lands collectively rather than individually was not agency action.[6]

Second, the Court held that the BLM's decision not to protect wildness areas from off-road vehicle use was not agency action.[7] Although the APA does define "agency action" to include an agency's "failure to act," the Court explained that the "failure to act" language applied only to those situations in which an agency failed to issue a specific "rule, order, license, sanction, [or other] relief" when required.[8]

b. Statutory Preclusion

Second, for a plaintiff to have a cause of action, judicial review cannot be precluded either explicitly or implicitly. Article III, Section 2 of the Federal Constitution grants Congress the power to regulate the jurisdiction of the federal courts, including the power to preclude judicial review altogether. Recognizing this fact, the APA provides that judicial review is available "except to the extent that ... [the] statute[ ] preclude[s] judicial review."[9] Express preclusion is relatively rare but does occur; implied preclusion is more common. Moreover, implied preclusion is more likely to arise on an exam because the law is not clear. Hence, we will focus our attention on implied preclusion.

---

4 APA § 551(13) (2012).

5 Lujan v. Defenders of Wildlife, 504 U.S. 555, 562 (1992).

6 *Id.* at 568.

7 Norton v. Southern Utah Wilderness Alliance, 542 U.S. 55, 67 (2004).

8 *Id.* at 62–63. *Compare,* Massachusetts v. EPA, 549 U.S. 497, 526 (2007) (holding that the EPA's denial of a rulemaking petition was agency action because the statute required the EPA to issue a rule).

9 APA § 701(a)(1) (2012).

A court will find that a particular statute impliedly precludes review when congressional intent to preclude review is "fairly discernible in the statutory scheme."[10] To determine whether congressional intent to preclude review is "fairly discernible in the statutory scheme," a court must determine first whether congressional intent to "allocate[ ] initial review to an administrative body" is "'fairly discernible" from the statute's language, structure, purpose, and legislative history.[11] If the court determines that Congress did not intend to preclude judicial review, then the court is finished: judicial review can proceed.[12]

If, instead, the court determines that Congress intended to preclude judicial review under this first step, then the court must ask three additional questions. The answers to these questions help the court determine which reviewing body would be more appropriate: a court or the agency. The three questions are the following: (1) would a finding of preclusion foreclose all meaningful judicial review, (2) is the federal suit wholly collateral to a statute's review provisions, and (3) are the claims outside of the agency's expertise.[13]

The Supreme Court has not been entirely clear regarding the relationship among these three questions and the "fairly discernible" step.[14] Must a court answer yes to all three questions to overcome a finding that congressional intent to preclude review was "fairly discernible in the statutory scheme"? Or would answering yes to any one question be sufficient? The Supreme Court's most recent case to address implied preclusion in any detail was *Elgin v. Department of the Treasury*.[15] In *Elgin*, the Court first found that congressional intent to preclude review was "fairly discernible in the statutory scheme."[16] The Court then thoroughly examined each factor independently, concluding that none were present to hold that preclusion was warranted.[17] Thus, it appears that if a court were to answer any one of the three questions with a "yes," then the court should find that it can hear the case, meaning implied preclusion is unwarranted.

---

[10]   Block v. Cmty. Nutrition Inst., 467 U.S. 340, 349, 351 (1984).

[11]   Thunder Basin Coal Co. v. Reich, 510 U.S. 200, 207 (1994) (quoting *Block*, 467 U.S. at 351).

[12]   *See e.g.*, *Block*, 467 U.S. at 345 (holding that Congress intended to preclude review for consumer litigants in the Agricultural Marketing Agreement Act).

[13]   *Thunder Basin*, 510 U.S. at 212–13.

[14]   *See, e.g.*, Free Enterprise Fund v. Public Co. Accounting Oversight Bd., 561 U.S. 477, 489–90 (2010) (examining the factors in a conclusory fashion).

[15]   567 U.S. 1 (2012).

[16]   *Id.* at 12.

[17]   *Id.* at 16.

c.   Committed to Agency Discretion

Third, for a plaintiff to have a cause of action, the plaintiff must be able to demonstrate that Congress did not leave the decision entirely to the agency, because the APA precludes courts from reviewing agency actions that are "committed to agency discretion by law."[18] What does "committed to agency discretion by law" mean? Occasionally, Congress confers such broad discretion on an agency that the courts would be unable to determine whether the agency abused its discretion when exercising its delegated authority. In such situations, the courts would have no meaningful standard against which to judge the agency's exercise of discretion,"[19] or "no law to apply."[20] Note that if the plaintiff files multiple claims, only the claim that is committed to agency discretion is non-reviewable.[21]

B.   The Plaintiff

We now turn from the court and the claim to the plaintiff. To determine who can bring a lawsuit against an agency, courts use the standing doctrine. There are two aspects to standing: constitutional standing and prudential standing. The standing doctrine is an incoherent doctrine. The Supreme Court's holdings are inconsistent in this area. The Court has generously interpreted constitutional standing when it wants to reach the merits of a case and ungenerously interpreted constitutional standing when it does not want to reach the merits. You can anticipate that you will likely be tested on this topic.

1.   Constitutional Standing Requirements

The Constitution restricts the power of the federal courts to hear only "cases and controversies."[22] The Supreme Court has interpreted this phrase to require plaintiffs to have a personal stake in the outcome of their case.[23] To demonstrate that their stake is personal, plaintiffs must show three things: (1) injury in fact, (2) causation, and (3) redressability.[24] We address each element below.

---

[18]   APA § 701(a)(2) (2012).

[19]   Heckler v. Chaney, 470 U.S. 821, 831 (1985).

[20]   Citizens to Preserve Overton Park v. Volpe, 401 U.S. 402, 410 (1971).

[21]   Webster v. Doe, 486 U.S. 592, 603–04 (1988) (holding that while a statutory claim was unreviewable, the constitutional claim remained valid).

[22]   U.S. CONST. art. III § 2, cl. 1.

[23]   See Allen v. Wright, 468 U.S. 737, 750 (1984) (holding that parents of a public school student lacked standing to sue to force schools to integrate).

[24]   Lujan, 504 U.S. at 560–61.

a.   Injury in Fact

First a plaintiff must show *injury in fact*. When an agency does something directly to a regulated entity—by revoking a license, imposing a fine, requiring specific labeling—that entity suffers a direct, economic injury. In these cases, injury in fact is easily met. When an agency acts less directly on a regulated entity—by approving a ski resort in a national park, defining "organic foods" to allow for some pesticides—the plaintiff will have a harder time demonstrating injury in fact because he or she may not be uniquely affected.

To show injury in fact, the plaintiff must demonstrate that he or she has a concrete, particularized, and imminent injury.[25] The injury can be economic, aesthetic, environmental, recreational, or informational.[26] Importantly, a plaintiff cannot establish injury in fact by complaining that the agency failed to follow a statutorily required procedure, like completing an environmental impact statement.[27] A plaintiff cannot establish in jury in fact in such a case because commonly all citizens are affected identically when an agency fails to follow a statutorily required procedure. Thus, the plaintiff would need to show that the agency's failure to follow the required procedure injured (concrete) or will injure (imminent) the plaintiff in a unique way (particularized). Note also that a threatened injury "must be *certainly impending* to constitute injury in fact, and ... allegations of *possible* future injury are not sufficient."[28]

In addition to demonstrating injury in fact, plaintiffs must demonstrate two other elements: causation and redressability.

b.   Causation

Second, to establish constitutional standing a plaintiff must demonstrate that the injury in fact was *caused by*, or is *fairly traceable to*, the agency action that the plaintiff is challenging as wrong. Specifically, plaintiffs must establish that the injury alleged

---

[25]   *Id.* at 572–73 (finding that standing was missing when the plaintiffs did not have immediate and concrete plans to observe various animal species in the wild).

[26]   *Massachusetts*, 549 U.S. at 521 (2007) (environmental injury); Friends of the Earth, Inc. v. Laidlaw Envtl. Servs., 528 U.S. 167, 183–84 (2000) (fear of physical harm); Bennett v. Spear, 520 U.S. 154, 161–62 (1997) (economic injury); United States v. Students Challenging Regulatory Agency Procedures, 412 U.S. 669, 699 (1973) (recreational and aesthetic injury); FEC v. Akins, 524 U.S. 11, 19 (1998) (informational injury); *Lujan*, 504 U.S. at 555 (aesthetic injury); Association of Data Processing v. Camp, 397 U.S. 150, 151 (1970) (economic injury).

[27]   *Lujan*, 504 U.S. at 573, n.8.

[28]   Clapper v. Amnesty Int'l USA, 568 U.S. 398, 409 (2013).

is "fairly traceable" to the agency's action. To determine whether the injury is fairly traceable, ask whether the plaintiff's injury resulted from the agency's decision to act or not act or whether the injury resulted from the actions of a third party.

For direct injuries, like a fine or loss of a license, a plaintiff will have no difficulty establishing causation. In contrast, a plaintiff will have difficulty establishing causation when the plaintiff alleges that the agency's action induced a third party to cause the harm.[29]

c. Redressability

Third, to establish constitutional standing a plaintiff must demonstrate not only that the injury in fact was caused by, or is fairly traceable to, the agency action that is being challenged, but also that a favorable court decision will likely *redress* that injury, remedying the plaintiff's harm. In other words, even if the plaintiff gets what he or she wants (*e.g.*, immediate implementation, rather than delay of a rule), would this result redress the alleged injury? If not, the plaintiff cannot demonstrate redressability.

Courts often address causation and redressability simultaneously, failing to separate the two elements. When an agency action causes injury, a favorable court decision will almost always redress the injury, so, courts have little to discuss. In contrast, a plaintiff will have difficulty demonstrating redressability when the plaintiff alleges that the agency's action induced a third party to cause the harm.[30]

2. Prudential Standing Requirements

Even if a plaintiff meets the constitutional standing requirements, courts retain the discretion to dismiss a complaint on prudential standing grounds. Because prudential standing requirements are not constitutionally based, Congress can alter them by statute.

There are two prudential standing issues: (1) standing for individualized, not generalized, grievances, and (2) standing for associations. We turn to each of these doctrines.

---

[29] *See, e.g.*, Simon v. Eastern Ky. Welfare Rights Org. (EKWRO), 426 U.S. 26, 42 (1976) (rejecting standing to a welfare rights organization that sued claiming an IRS regulation would cause hospitals to reduce medical care for indigent people); *Allen*, 468 U.S. at 757 (holding that the parents of African-American children could not demonstrate causation regarding the impact of a tax regulation because the schools were an independent third party not before the court); *compare Bennett*, 520 U.S. at 169–70 (finding that causation was met where one agency was required to follow another agency's recommendation).

[30] *Allen*, 468 U.S. at 758–59.

One prudential concern is that courts prefer not to hear lawsuits addressing injuries shared by many citizens in the same way. For example, an illegal public expenditure injures all citizens because the money comes from a treasury to which all citizens contribute. Additionally, all citizens have an interest in the government's obligation to follow the law in general. Yet courts are reluctant to use such wide-spread and generally shared injuries as the basis for finding standing likely because the legislature is a more appropriate forum for addressing generalized grievances. In any event, courts require plaintiffs to have an individualized injury. An individualized injury is one that affects the plaintiff or plaintiffs in a more personal and individual way.[31]

A second prudential concern is that third parties generally cannot sue to enforce the rights of others. Yet, interest groups and associations, like the Sierra Club, often have more resources to mount better legal challenges and are more likely to sue in the public interest than individuals. Thus, the Supreme Court has developed a doctrine to allow these interest groups to sue on behalf of individuals and entities who meet the constitutional standing requirements. Be aware that standing questions on exams commonly address associational standing.

To have standing, interest groups must show three things. First, they must show that one or more of their members have constitutional standing, meaning the member can demonstrate injury in fact, causation, and redressability (all addressed in the last section).

Second, the interest group must show that the group's purpose relates to the issues in the lawsuit, meaning that an environmental group can sue to enforce the environmental concerns of its members while a labor union cannot.

Third, the interest group must show that the presence of individual members is not needed in the litigation, meaning, simply, that no monetary relief is sought, just injunctive and declaratory relief.[32] Once the interest group has established standing, the group can "argue the public interest to support the claim that the agency failed to comply with its statutory mandate."[33]

---

[31] *See Massachusetts*, 549 U.S. at 526 (holding that Massachusetts had standing to sue the Environmental Protection Agency to regulate greenhouse gas emissions because its coastline would be uniquely affected).

[32] Hunt v. Washington Apple Adv. Comm'n, 432 U.S. 333, 342 (1977).

[33] *Sierra Club*, 405 U.S. at 737.

3.   Statutory Standing Requirements: Zone of Interests

In addition to the constitutional and prudential standing requirements, there is an additional standing requirement that comes from APA § 702 known as the zone of interests test. You should be aware, however, that some courts consider the zone of interests test a part of prudential standing.

Section 702 of the APA provides: "a person . . . adversely affected or aggrieved by agency action *within the meaning of a relevant statute*, is entitled to judicial review thereof."[34] The italicized language limits standing to persons who are "arguably" within the zone of interests the statute protects or regulates. For example, a statute addressing postal routes protects and regulates postal routes, not postal employee jobs.[35] While the courts generously interpreted this requirement in the past, more recently, they have been less generous.[36]

4.   Standing Requirements: Summary

The following chart summarizes these standing doctrines:

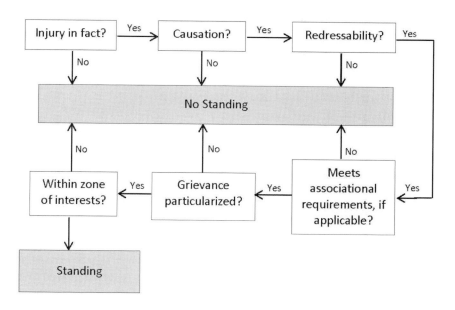

---

[34]   APA § 702 (emphasis added).

[35]   *Air Courier Conference v. American Postal Workers Union*, 498 U.S. 517, 530 (1991) (holding that a union representing postal workers did not have statutory standing because the employees' interests were not within the zone of interests that the postal act was designed to protect).

[36]   *See e.g., Ass'n of Data Processing*, 397 U.S. at 153 (holding that data-processing services were within the zone of interest of a statute that allowed banks to provide data-process services).

C. The Timing

We now turn from the plaintiff to timing. There are three doctrines regarding the timing of judicial review: finality, exhaustion, and ripeness. Each of these three doctrines serves different purposes. The finality doctrine respects the right of the agency to complete its work before courts intervene and use judicial resources that may be unnecessary. The exhaustion doctrine respects the right of the agency to correct its own mistakes before courts intervene. The ripeness doctrine respects the need of the courts to have the issues in the case sufficiently developed for judicial review. However, these doctrines do not have clear boundaries; there is overlap.

1. Finality

Courts only review decisions that are "final" because the function of a reviewing court is to "review" not to "decide" issues.[37] Finality is a common law doctrine derived from Article III's case or controversy requirement. It was codified in section 704 of the APA, which provides that *"final* agency action for which there is no other adequate remedy" is subject to judicial review.[38]

In examining whether an agency action is final, courts focus on two questions: "First, the action must mark the 'consummation' of the agency's decisionmaking process—it must not be of a merely tentative or interlocutory nature. And second, the action must be one by which 'rights or obligations have been determined,' or from which 'legal consequences will flow.' "[39] The first question focuses on the agency's actions to see whether the agency has reached the end of its decisionmaking process. The second question focuses on the impact of that action on the plaintiff; how directly will the complaining plaintiff be affected?

Pursuant to the first question, a court must determine whether the agency action challenged is the culmination of the agency's process. For adjudication and legislative rulemaking, the question of whether the agency has completed its decisionmaking process is less commonly unclear or disputed. However, for non-legislative

---

[37] *See* Rochester Tele. Corp v. Unites States, 307 U.S. 125, 131 (1939) (explaining that the finality doctrine is routed in Article III's case or controversy requirement).

[38] APA § 704 (2012) (emphasis added).

[39] *Bennett,* 520 U.S. at 177–78 (citations omitted); *accord* Franklin v. Massachusetts, 505 U.S. 788, 797 (1992) (stating that the Court must look to whether the agency has completed its decisionmaking process and whether the result of that process is one that will directly affect the parties).

rulemaking, the question of whether the agency has completed its decisionmaking process is more commonly disputed.[40]

Pursuant to the second question, a court must decide whether the agency's action affects the plaintiff in a concrete way. The Court has provided varying articulations of this question, sometimes requiring that legal consequences flow, more often requiring that the plaintiff suffer some direct effect.[41] Because non-legislative rules generally are not ones from which legal consequences will flow, the Court's articulation may differ depending on the type of action being challenged.

2. Exhaustion

The next timing doctrine is exhaustion. For non-APA actions, the common law exhaustion doctrine applies.[42] The common law doctrine provides that courts should not review an agency action unless and until the plaintiff has exhausted any remedies available from the agency itself. There are three exceptions to the common law exhaustion requirement: First, a plaintiff need not exhaust administrative remedies when the administrative remedy would undermine the ability of the courts to provide effective relief.[43] For example, a plaintiff need not exhaust administrative remedies when agency relief will be unreasonably delayed or the injury needs immediate relief if any relief is to be had at all.[44]

Second, a plaintiff need not exhaust administrative remedies when the administrative remedy would be inadequate because the

---

[40] Compare, Nat'l Automatic Laundry & Cleaning Council v. Shultz, 443 F.2d 689, 702 (D.C. Cir. 1971) (holding that an opinion letter was final agency action because the agency head had issued the letter and it applied to an entire industry), with Taylor-Callahan-Coleman Cntys. Dist. Adult Prob. Dep't v. Dole, 948 F.2d 953, 960 (5th Cir. 1991) (holding that an opinion letter was not final agency action because the letter was directed only to a particular local government and not to all local governments).

[41] See, e.g., Bennett, 520 U.S. at 178 (test whether "rights or obligations have been determined," or from which "legal consequences will flow"); Dalton v. Specter, 511 U.S. 462, 470 (1994) (test whether action "will directly affect the parties"); Darby v. Cisneros, 509 U.S. 137, 144 (1993) (test whether there is "actual, concrete injury"); Franklin, 505 U.S. at 797 (test whether agency's action has a "direct effect on" the plaintiff): Abbott Labs, 387 U.S. at 149 (test whether the "effects are felt in a concrete way").

[42] See, e.g., McCarthy v. Madigan, 503 U.S. 140, 145–46 (1992).

[43] See, e.g., Walker v. Southern Ry. Co., 385 U.S. 196, 198 (1966) (finding a possible delay of ten years in an administrative proceeding made exhaustion unnecessary).

[44] See, e.g., Bowen v. New York, 476 U.S. 467, 483 (1986) (waiving exhaustion for disability claimants); Moore v. East Cleveland, 431 U.S. 494, 497, n.5 (1977) (determining exhaustion is not required of a criminal defendant when the statute in question did not mandate exhaustion of remedies prior to judicial review).

agency cannot provide the requested relief.[45] Third, a plaintiff need not exhaust administrative remedies when the administrative agency is biased or prejudiced against the plaintiff such that exhaustion would be futile.[46]

However, for APA actions, Congress codified the exhaustion doctrine in APA § 704. That section provides:

> Except as otherwise expressly required by statute, agency action otherwise final is final whether or not there has been . . . any form of reconsideration . . . unless the agency otherwise requires by rule and provides that the action meanwhile is inoperative.[47]

Thus, exhaustion is required in two situations only: (1) when a statute expressly requires exhaustion, and (2) when an agency's own rule requires exhaustion *and* the agency stays its action pending the appeal.[48] Note that under § 704, exhaustion is the exception, whereas at common law, exhaustion is required. Finally, while the Court has not yet said so explicitly, the exceptions to the common law exhaustion doctrine likely do not apply to lawsuits brought under the APA because § 704 does not include any such exceptions.

3. *Ripeness*

The third timing doctrine is ripeness, which differs from exhaustion. Exhaustion is the appropriate doctrine to apply when a plaintiff could have tried to address his or her concerns with the agency directly but chose not to. In contrast, ripeness is the appropriate doctrine to apply when there was no way for the plaintiff to address his or her concerns with the agency first, such as when a final regulation is challenged pre-enforcement.

Unlike finality and exhaustion, the ripeness doctrine is not codified in the APA. Hence, its development and application comes from case law. Ripeness issues usually arise when a plaintiff challenges an agency rulemaking, rather than adjudication, and seeks pre-enforcement review.

---

[45]   *McCarthy*, 503 U.S. at 156–58 (Rehnquist J., concurring) (stating that exhaustion should not be required when the petitioner sought monetary damages that the agency had no authority to grant); *Moore*, 431 U.S. at 497, n.5 (concluding it would be "wholly inappropriate" to require criminal defendants to exhaust of administrative remedies).

[46]   Houghton v. Shafer, 392 U.S. 639, 640 (1968) (stating that requiring exhaustion would be a futile act).

[47]   APA § 704.

[48]   *See Darby*, 509 U.S. at 148 (holding that the plaintiff did not need to exhaust administrative remedies because neither the relevant statute nor the regulation required exhaustion).

To determine whether a case is ripe, a court must "evaluate both [1] the fitness of the issues for judicial decision and [2] the hardship to the parties of withholding court consideration."[49] The first factor requires the court to determine whether the issues are legal or factual questions; legal questions do not benefit from further factual development. The second factor requires the court to determine whether the plaintiff will actually be harmed if judicial review is delayed.

Applying these factors, courts typically find cases to be ripe when plaintiffs challenge agency regulations that require entities to change their behavior, to comply with new duties, or to abide by new restrictions.[50] In contrast, when agency regulations do not require regulated entities to make immediate changes, courts typically find challenges to them unripe.[51]

4. Timing Requirements: Summary

Finality, exhaustion, and ripeness are related doctrines, resolution of which turns on the consideration of similar factors; hence, courts sometimes carelessly interchange them. However, their focus is different; focusing on these differences on your exam will help you keep them straight.

Finality focuses on whether the agency has finished its work so the records will be complete and the judiciary will not waste its time on moot issues. The beneficiary of finality is the court because finality ensures that the court will have a complete record with a non-mooted case before it.

Exhaustion focuses on whether there are means of review or redress available within the agency. The beneficiary of exhaustion is the agency because exhaustion ensures that the agency's internal review processes will be followed before the courts intrude into the process.

Ripeness focuses on the issues to be decided and the degree to which those issues have reached the state of development and refinement that will permit a court to make a decision about their legality. The beneficiary of ripeness is the court, because ripeness protects the court from inserting itself into a speculative or abstract question.

---

[49]   *Abbott Labs,* 387 U.S. at 149.

[50]   *See, e.g., Id.* at 149; *Nat'l Automatic Laundry,* 443 F.2d at 689 (finding ripe a challenge to an agency opinion letter regarding hour and wage requirements).

[51]   *See, e.g.,* Toilet Goods Ass'n v. Gardner, 387 U.S. 158, 160–61 (1967); Florida Power & Light Co. v. EPA, 145 F.3d 1414, 1421 (D.C. Cir. 1998) (finding unripe challenges to an agency's interpretation of its authority, which were contained in a preamble to a proposed rulemaking).

AVAILABILITY CHECKLIST

A. Jurisdiction—

1. Does the enabling statute give federal courts jurisdiction?

    a. **No**—If no, then jurisdiction must be found based on the federal question statute, 28 U.S.C. § 1331. The APA does not provide jurisdiction. <u>Proceed to A.1.2. below</u>.

    b. **Yes**—If yes, then the court has jurisdiction. <u>Proceed to B. below</u> to see if the plaintiff has a cause of action.

2. Does the plaintiff allege a claim that "aris[es] under the Constitution, law, or treaties of the United States"?

    a. **No**—If no, then the court does not have jurisdiction. <u>Stop here</u>. But this answer is likely wrong because most challenges to agency action will involve questions about federal law.

    b. **Yes**—If yes, then the court has jurisdiction. <u>Proceed to B. below</u> to see if the plaintiff has a cause of action.

B. Cause of Action—

1. Does the enabling statute provide that anyone adversely affected by the agency's action may file an action challenging its validity or otherwise provide a cause of action?

    a. **No**—If no, then the enabling statute does not provide a cause of action, but the APA may. <u>Proceed to B.2. below</u>.

    b. **Yes**—If yes, then the plaintiff has a cause of action. <u>Proceed to C. below</u> to see if the plaintiff has standing.

2. Does APA § 702 provide the plaintiff with a cause of action?

    a. **Agency Action**—Did the agency either act in a discrete manner or fail to act when required to act?

        i. **No**—If no, then there is no agency action. <u>Stop here</u>.

ii. **Yes**—If yes, then there was agency action. Proceed to B.2.b. to determine whether the statute precludes review implicitly or explicitly.

b. **Statutory Preclusion—**

i. Does the statute explicitly preclude the court from reviewing plaintiff(s)'s claim?

(a). **No**—If no, then Congress did not explicitly precluded review but may have implicitly precluded review. Proceed to B.2.b.ii.

(b). **Yes**—If yes, then the court cannot hear the case. Stop here. But this answer is likely wrong because Congress rarely precludes review explicitly.

ii. Is it fairly discernible in the statutory scheme (meaning the statute's language, structure, purpose, and legislative history) that Congress implicitly precluded the federal courts from reviewing plaintiff's claim?

(a). **No**—If no, then Congress did not implicitly preclude review. Proceed to B.2.c. to determine whether the issue is committed to agency discretion.

(b). **Yes**—If yes, then ask (1) would a finding of preclusion foreclose all meaningful judicial review, (2) is the federal suit wholly collateral to a statute's review provisions, and (3) are the claims outside of the agency's expertise?

— **Yes**—If you answered yes to any of these questions, then Congress did not implicitly preclude review. Proceed to B.2.c. to determine whether the issue is committed to agency discretion

— **No**—If you answered no to all of the questions, then Congress precluded review, and the court cannot hear the case. Stop here.

c. **Committed to Agency Discretion**—Does the statute provide meaningful standards with which to measure the agency's action?

i.   No—If no, then Congress committed this particular decision to the agency, and the court cannot hear the case (assuming that is the only challenge). <u>Stop here</u>. But this answer is likely wrong because judicial review is preferred.

ii.   Yes—If yes, then the plaintiff has a cause of action that the court can hear. <u>Proceed to C.</u> to determine whether the plaintiff(s) has standing.

C. Standing—

1. **Prudential Standing**—Is the plaintiff an association suing on behalf of the public rather than for its own personal injury?

   a.   No—If no, then plaintiff must be suing directly (whether it is the association suing for its own harm or a plaintiff suing for his/her/its own harm). Associational standing is irrelevant. <u>Proceed to C.2. below</u> to determine whether the plaintiff has constitutional standing.

   b.   Yes—If yes, then the plaintiff must meet the associational standing requirements. <u>Proceed to C.1.c. below</u>.

   c.   Associational Standing—

   i.   Assuming an association is suing, does the lawsuit relate to the purposes of the association?

   (a). No—If no, then the association has no standing pursuant to prudential standing. <u>Stop here</u>. But this answer is likely wrong because associations generally only sue for issues related to their mission.

   (b). Yes—If yes, then the association meets one element of associational standing. <u>Proceed to C.1.c.ii. below</u> to see if the association meets the other elements.

   ii. Assuming an association is suing, can the lawsuit proceed without an individual's participation, meaning that the lawsuit is for injunctive or declaratory relief only?

   (a). No—If no, then the association has no standing pursuant to prudential standing. <u>Stop here</u>. But this answer is likely wrong because associations generally only sue for declaratory and injunctive relief.

(b). Yes—If yes, then the association meets another element of associational standing. Proceed to C.1.c.iii. below to see if the association meets the remaining element.

iii. Assuming an association is suing, does one member have constitutional standing, meaning injury in fact, causation, and redressability? (you will need to work through C.2. below, then return here).

(a). No—If no, then the association has no standing pursuant to prudential standing. Stop here.

(b). Yes—If yes, then the association meets the prudential standing requirements. Proceed to C.3. below to see if the plaintiff meets the statutory standing requirements.

2. **Constitutional Standing—**

a. **Injury in Fact**—Can the plaintiff show unique injury?

i. Does the plaintiff allege that he or she would be directly injured economically (*e.g.*, by a fine) or physically by the agency?

(a). No—If no, then plaintiff must be alleging an indirect injury. Proceed to C.2.a.ii. below.

(b). Yes—If yes, the plaintiff has an injury in fact that is concrete and particularized, which is one element of constitutional standing. Proceed to C.2.b. below to determine whether plaintiff can show causation.

ii. Does the plaintiff allege only that he or she suffered a procedural injury, meaning the agency failed to follow a legally required procedure?

(a). No—If no, then plaintiff must be alleging a different indirect injury. Proceed to C.2.a.iii. below.

(b). Yes—If yes, the plaintiff does not have injury in fact, which is one element of constitutional standing. <u>Stop here</u>.

iii. Does the plaintiff allege that he or she suffered an informational injury, meaning the agency failed to disclose information it was required to disclose to this plaintiff?

(a). No—If no, then plaintiff must be alleging a different indirect injury. <u>Proceed to C.2.a.iv. below</u>.

(b). Yes—If yes, then plaintiff has injury in fact. <u>Proceed to C.2.b. below</u> to determine whether plaintiff can show causation.

iv. Does the plaintiff allege that he or she suffered a recreational, aesthetic, or environmental injury?

(a). No—If no, then the plaintiff does not have injury in fact, which is one element of constitutional standing. <u>Stop here</u>. This answer is likely wrong; plaintiff must be alleging one of the injuries above.

(b). Yes—If yes, then ask whether the plaintiff can show concrete plans to visit the location or see the nature to be harmed in the near future?

— **No**—If no, then the plaintiff does not have injury in fact, which is one element of constitutional standing. <u>Stop here</u>.

— **Yes**—If yes, then plaintiff has injury in fact. <u>Proceed to C.2.b. below</u> to see if the plaintiff can show causation.

b. Causation—Can the plaintiff show that the alleged illegal action by the agency caused the plaintiff's harm?

i. No—If no, then the harm was likely caused by a third party, and plaintiff cannot show causation, which is one element of constitutional standing. <u>Stop here</u>.

ii. Yes—If yes, then the plaintiff can show causation. <u>Proceed to C.2.c. below</u> to determine whether plaintiff can show redressability.

   c. **Redressability**—Can the plaintiff show that a favorable decision will remedy the plaintiff's harm?

    i. **No**—If no, then the harm cannot be remedied by the agency, and the plaintiff cannot show redressability, which is one element of constitutional standing. <u>Stop here.</u>

    ii. **Yes**—If yes, the plaintiff can show redressability, which is one element of constitutional standing. <u>Proceed to C.3. below</u> to determine whether plaintiff meets statutory standing requirements.

3. **Statutory Standing (Zone of Interests)**—Is plaintiff bringing suit pursuant to APA § 702?

   a. **No**—If no, then the plaintiff must be bringing suit pursuant to the enabling statute, the zone of interest requirement does not apply because the plaintiff must be within the protection of the relevant statute. <u>Proceed to D. below</u> to determine whether plaintiff's lawsuit meets the timing requirements.

   b. **Yes**—If yes, then the plaintiff must demonstrate that he/she/it is "arguably" within the zone of interests the specific statute was meant to protect. Can plaintiff meet this burden?

    i. **No**—If no, then the plaintiff cannot meet statutory standing requirements. <u>Stop here.</u>

    ii. **Yes**—If yes, the plaintiff can meet the statutory standing requirements. <u>Proceed to D. below</u> to determine whether plaintiff's lawsuit meets the timing requirements.

D. **Timing—**

1. Is the plaintiff suing pursuant to APA § 704?

   a. **No**—If no, then the common law doctrine of finality, exhaustion, and ripeness may apply. <u>Stop here</u> and apply those doctrines. But in an Administrative Law course, it is more likely that you will be tested on these doctrines as codified in APA § 704.

   b. **Yes**—If yes, then <u>proceed to D.2. below</u> to determine whether now is the appropriate time for a court to hear the plaintiff's claim.

2. **Finality—**

    a. Is the action the culmination of the agency's decisionmaking process?

       i. **No**—if no, then the agency's action is not final, and the court cannot hear the case at this time. Stop here.

       ii. **Yes**—If yes, then the agency's action meets one of the finality elements. Proceed to D.2.b. below to see if it meets the other.

    b. Is the agency action one from which "rights or obligations have been determined,' or from which 'legal consequences will flow?' "

       i. **No**—if no, then the agency's action is not final, and the court cannot hear the case at this time. Stop here.

       ii. **Yes**—If yes, then the agency's action is final. Proceed to D.3. below to see if the plaintiff meets the exhaustion requirements.

3. **Exhaustion—**

    a. Does the enabling statute expressly require the plaintiff to exhaust administrative remedies?

       i. **No**—If no, then the statute does not require the plaintiff to exhaust administrative remedies. Proceed to D.3.b. below to determine whether a regulation requires the plaintiff to exhaust administrative remedies.

       ii. **Yes**—If yes, then the plaintiff must exhaust administrative remedies prior to filing suit. You may wish to note here that the common law exceptions to exhaustion likely to do not apply because Congress did not codify them within APA § 704. Stop here.

    b. Does the agency's own regulation expressly require the plaintiff to exhaust administrative remedies and stay its action pending administrative appeal?

       i. **No**—If no, then the regulation does not require the plaintiff to exhaust administrative remedies. Proceed to D.4. below to determine whether the action is ripe.

    ii. **Yes**—If yes, then the plaintiff must exhaust administrative remedies prior to filing suit. You may wish to note here that the common law exceptions to exhaustion likely to do not apply because Congress did not codify them within APA § 704. Stop here.

4. **Ripeness**— Is the case sufficiently developed for judicial review?

    a. Does the case involve purely legal issues?

        i. **No**—If no, then the case is not ripe, and the court should not hear it at this time. Stop here.

        ii. **Yes**—If yes, then the case meets one of the ripeness elements. Proceed to D.4.b. below to determine whether case meets both elements.

    b. Will the plaintiff actually be harmed if judicial review is delayed?

        i. **No**—If no, then the case is not ripe, and the court should not hear it at this time. Stop here.

        ii. **Yes**—If yes, then the case if ripe for judicial review at this time. Proceed to Chapter 7 to determine the appropriate standard of review the court will apply.

ILLUSTRATIVE PROBLEMS

■ PROBLEM 6.1 ■

Environmental and other public interest groups can sue on behalf of their members' injuries. What must such a group show to establish standing?

Analysis

This issue in this problem is how to establish associational standing. Using the checklist above (C), you should ask (1) whether the lawsuit relates to the purposes of the association; (2) whether the lawsuit can proceed without an individual's participation, meaning that the lawsuit is for injunctive or declaratory relief only; and whether one member would have constitutional standing, meaning injury in fact, causation, and redressability. The member's required injury need not be financial, but can involve injury to environmental, aesthetic, or recreational interests.[52]

---

[52] Sierra Club v. Morton, 405 U.S. 727, 734 (1972).

■ **PROBLEM 6.2** ■

Assume that Congress authorized the Department of Education (DOE) to administer a new federal student loan program. The DOE promulgated regulations using notice-and-comment procedures that were in effect for twenty years. These original regulations defined student eligibility. DOE has decided to change the eligibility requirements, which will make it more difficult for students to obtain student loans in the future. Specifically, DOE plans to lower the amount of family income a student may have access to before that student may qualify for a loan. DOE issues the new regulation after notice-and-comment. All loans already awarded will continue in force. After the notice-and-comment period, the DOE promulgates the new regulation, which will take effect the following year.

A student received a loan under DOE's original regulations. That loan will continue without change. But if the student were to apply for another loan, the student would be denied because his family income would be too high to qualify. The student sues to enjoin the DOE from enforcing its new regulation, claiming that DOE has misinterpreted language in the statute. Would judicial review be available? The statute is silent regarding exhaustion, and there are no relevant agency rules on exhaustion.

Analysis

The issue in this problem is whether the student meets all of the availability requirements. Using the checklist above (A.1.), you should ask first whether a federal court would have jurisdiction over this particular claim. In this case, the relevant statute does not appear to grant the federal court jurisdiction, the APA does not grant jurisdiction; hence, jurisdiction must be found based on the federal question statute, 28 U.S.C. § 1331. The student is alleging a claim that arises under a statute of the United States, the federal student loan program; thus, the court would have jurisdiction.

Second, you should determine whether the enabling statute gives the student the right to sue ("a cause of action"). Here, the enabling statute does not provide that anyone adversely affected by the agency's action may file an action challenging its validity or otherwise provide a cause of action; hence, you should turn to the APA to see if it provides the plaintiff with a cause of action. To determine whether the APA § 702 provides the student with a cause of action, you should determine that the agency acted in a discrete manner—it issued a regulation. Therefore, there was agency action. Next, you would note that there are no facts suggesting that the statute either explicitly or implicitly precludes judicial review. Finally, you would note that there are no facts suggesting that the statute does not provide meaningful standards with which to measure the agency's action, meaning Congress did not commit this particular decision to the agency. Thus, the plaintiff has a cause of action under the APA.

Third, you must determine whether the student has standing to bring this claim: prudential, constitutional, and statutory. The student is not an association, so associational standing requirements are not applicable, and the grievance is particularized.

As for constitutional standing, the student must demonstrate injury in fact, causation, and redressability. In this case, while the student has not yet been harmed by the regulation, were it to be enacted, the student would be economically harmed because the amount of his federal aid would likely be reduced. Injury in fact is thus met. Moreover, the student would likely be able to show that by changing the eligibility requirements, the DOE's allegedly illegal action will cause the harm and that a favorable decision would remedy the plaintiff's harm. The agency is causing the harm, not a third party. Hence, constitutional standing is likely met.

As for statutory standing, the student is likely to be able to demonstrate that he or she is "arguably" within the zone of interests of the federal student loan program statute. Hence, statutory standing is likely met.

Fourth, you must determine whether the student can bring this particular claim at this particular time. The student would be suing pursuant to the APA, so section 704's finality and exhaustion requirements apply (ripeness is a common law doctrine and also applies). Regarding finality, a final regulation is the culmination of the agency's decisionmaking process and the change in the eligibility change is one from which rights will be determined or legal consequences will flow. Hence, finality is met. Regarding exhaustion, the statute does not require the student to exhaust administrative remedies, and there is no relevant administrative regulation. Hence, exhaustion is met.

Regarding ripeness, you must analyze (1) whether the plaintiff's claims are purely legal, and (2) whether the plaintiff would be harmed if judicial review were delayed. Here, the student's claims involve purely legal issues, namely the interpretation of language in the statute. No factual develop is necessary to resolve that question. However, delay will not harm the student. This suit would involve pre-enforcement review because the regulation is not yet in effect. Here, the student has not yet applied for a loan and been denied. The student may never apply for the loan. Hence, the case is not yet ripe, and the court should not hear it at this time.

POINTS TO REMEMBER

- Judicial review is not always available, due to certain judge-made doctrines and constitutional limitations.

- Courts must have jurisdiction over the plaintiff's claim. Such jurisdiction comes from the agency's enabling statute or from federal question jurisdiction. It does not come from the APA.

- The statute must provide plaintiff with a cause of action. If it does not include one, the APA does.

- Congress can preclude review, explicitly or implicitly.

- Congress may grant agencies complete discretion, in which case courts will have no "law to apply."

- Courts must have jurisdiction over the plaintiff, meaning that the plaintiff must have standing: constitutional, prudential, and statutory.

- For a plaintiff to have constitutional standing, the plaintiff must have an injury in fact, which is concrete and particularized, which is caused by the agency action challenged, and which is redressable by a favorable court decision.

- For a plaintiff to have prudential standing, the plaintiff must generally assert its own claims and those claims must be particularized.

- An association may assert claims on behalf of its members if one of its members has constitutional standing, the association's purpose are related to the issues, and the lawsuit seeks only declaratory or injunctive relief so that the individual member's participation is unnecessary.

- For a plaintiff to have statutory standing under the APA, the plaintiff must "arguably" be within the zone of interests of the relevant statute.

- Courts only review final agency actions, when administrative remedies have been exhausted (if required) and when the actions are ripe enough to present issues clear enough for judicial resolution.

CHAPTER 7

What Standard of Review Applies?

In the last chapter, you learned about the doctrines limiting a plaintiff's ability to obtain judicial review of an agency's action. Finally, in this chapter, you will learn what standard of review a court will apply to resolve a plaintiff's claims assuming the plaintiff is able to get into court. While I cannot guess in advance whether your professor will test you on rulemaking or adjudication, I can virtually guarantee that your professor will test you on the material in this chapter.

To determine the appropriate standard of review, you will need to ask two questions. First, what type of issue is the court reviewing: did the agency decide a question of fact, policy, or law? Second, how did the agency resolve that issue: did the agency use formal rulemaking, formal adjudication, notice-and-comment rulemaking, informal adjudication, or non-legislative rulemaking? After you have asked these two questions and determined the appropriate standard of review, you will then need to apply that standard of review to the facts of your case. This latter step is the one that students often omit on their exams. Do not make this mistake.

REVIEW

An agency's decision may be reviewed multiple times. When a court reviews a decision an agency reached as part of a formal adjudication process, for example, that decision may be reviewed three different times. First, the agency may review the administrative law judge's (ALJ) decision during an internal review process, using a *de novo* standard of review. Second, a court of appeals may review the agency's final order. Third, the Supreme Court may review the court of appeals' decision. This chapter addresses the second step, when an appellate court reviews an agency's final administrative order or, in the case of rulemaking, a regulation.

The enabling statute may provide the standard of review. If the statute does not include a standard of review, then APA § 706 contains default standard of review provisions. We will explore these provisions below. As noted above, the applicable standard of review under § 706 depends on the issue, or question, the agency resolved. There are four such questions: (1) questions of fact; (2) questions of discretion or policy; (3) questions of law; and (4) mixed questions of law and fact (otherwise known as questions of law application).[1]

A.   Defining Questions of Fact & Policy

1.   Questions of Fact

A question of fact is one in which the resolution of the question does not require an application of or knowledge of the law. The finding "is an assertion that a phenomenon has happened or is or will be happening independent of or anterior to any assertion as to its legal effect."[2] Findings of fact answer questions about who did what, to whom, and with what effect.

Let's consider a finding of fact made in a non-agency setting: a car accident. Assume that during the investigation, the accident investigator noted that the skid marks on the pavement were 46 feet long. This finding would be one of fact. The law is irrelevant.

Now let's turn to the agency setting. Agencies make factual determinations regularly. For example, an agency may have to determine whether a pesticide is dangerous. An agency may have to determine whether an employee was fired in the way she claimed or in the way her employer claimed. These questions are questions of fact.

What is the scope of review for a court reviewing an agency's finding of fact? APA § 706 provides two standards of review for agency findings of fact: (1) the substantial evidence standard for findings of fact made during *formal* proceedings, and (2) the arbitrary and capricious standard for findings of fact made during *informal* proceedings. Notice that the appropriate standard turns on the procedure the agency used to resolve its question of fact.

---

[1]   APA § 706 (2012).

[2]   LOUIS L. JAFFE, JUDICIAL CONTROL OF ADMINISTRATIVE ACTION 548 (1965).

2. Questions of Policy & Discretion

A question of policy involves an agency's application of the law to facts, usually made during rulemaking. Questions of policy generally arise during rulemakings rather than during adjudications because the relevant facts are not judicial facts (*e.g.*, who said what, did what, did it when); rather, the relevant facts are legislative in nature (*e.g.*, how much of a pesticide should be prohibited to make food safe).

Often, policy questions involve complex and controverted scientific and technical issues. For example, suppose an agency must decide on the location for a new highway, must determine how many parts per million of a certain chemical will be injurious to human health, must identify what kinds of safety features should be required in passenger cars, or must indicate what level of protection should be afforded workers in factories. These questions are all policy questions, involving complex and controverted legislative facts. To resolve such policy questions, the agency must consider the relevant legislative facts in light of its delegated authority, *e.g.* "to make drinking water safe." Commonly, the legislative facts do not clearly point in one direction, so the agency must use discretion to determine the best policy choice.

What is the scope of review for a court reviewing an agency's finding of policy? As with questions of fact, APA § 706 provides two standards of review: (1) the substantial evidence standard for findings made during *formal* proceedings, and (2) the arbitrary and capricious standard for findings made during *informal* proceedings. Again, notice that the appropriate standard turns on the procedure the agency used to resolve its question of policy. We examine these two standards next.

B. Standards of Review for Questions of Fact & Policy

1. Substantial Evidence

A reviewing court must use the "substantial evidence" standard to review the adequacy of an agency's findings of fact or findings of policy made during *formal* proceedings (adjudications or rulemakings required to be conducted on the record under APA § 556 and § 557).[3] Substantial evidence is commonly thought of as fairly deferential to the agency to recognize that the agency has expertise that the court does not.

---

[3]   APA § 706(2)(E) (2012).

Under the substantial evidence standard of review, a reviewing court should not substitute its judgment for that of the agency. The test has been defined as follows:

> [S]ubstantial evidence is more than a mere scintilla. It means such relevant evidence as a reasonable mind might accept as adequate to support a conclusion . . . . [I]t must do more than create a suspicion of the existence of the fact to be established. . . . [I]t must be enough to justify, if the trial were to a jury, a refusal to direct a verdict when the conclusion sought to be drawn from it is one of fact for the jury.[4]

Using this standard, a reviewing court should ask whether a reasonable person could make the same finding that the agency made after reviewing the evidence in the record. The court should examine each of the agency's findings of fact or policy to see if there is evidence in the record to support that finding. In doing so, the court must take into account not only the evidence supporting the agency's findings but also any evidence that "fairly detracts" from that finding.[5] A reviewing court's job is to decide whether the agency's findings are well-reasoned, not whether those findings are correct.

2. Arbitrary & Capricious

The substantial evidence standard is used to review the sufficiency of findings of fact or findings of policy made during *formal* proceedings or when Congress specifies this standard of review in the enabling statute. For reviewing the sufficiency of findings of fact and policy made during *informal* proceedings, the APA provides that the reviewing court shall hold unlawful and set aside agency findings that are "arbitrary, capricious, [or] an abuse of discretion."[6] These three terms do not have independent significance; rather, combined, they are understood to mean arbitrary and capricious review.

Historically, the arbitrary and capricious standard of review was viewed as providing overwhelming deference to agency findings. However, the Supreme Court gave the standard unexpected teeth in *Citizens to Preserve Overton Park, Inc. v. Volpe*,[7] describing it in the following way:

---

[4]   Universal Camera Corp. v. NLRB, 340 U.S. 474, 477 (1951) (internal citations omitted).

[5]   *Id.* at 487.

[6]   APA § 706(2)(A) (2012).

[7]   401 U.S. 402 (1971).

To make [a finding that the actual choice made was not "arbitrary, capricious, an abuse of discretion, or otherwise not in accordance with law"] the court must consider whether the decision was based on a consideration of the relevant factors and whether there has been a clear error of judgment. Although this inquiry into the facts is to be searching and careful, the ultimate standard of review is a narrow one. The court is not empowered to substitute its judgment for that of the agency.[8]

Thus, for arbitrary and capricious review, courts must review the administrative record that was before the agency when it made its findings to determine whether "the decision was based on a consideration of the relevant factors and whether there has been a clear error of judgment."[9]

In *Motor Vehicles Manufacturers Ass'n v. State Farm*,[10] the Supreme Court reviewed an agency's policy findings (that air bags and automatic seatbelts would not save enough lives to justify their cost). In doing so, the Court further explained the arbitrary and capricious standard of review:

[T]he agency must examine the relevant data and articulate a satisfactory explanation for its action including a rational connection between the facts found and the choice made. In reviewing that explanation, we must consider whether the decision was based on a consideration of the relevant factors and whether there has been a clear error of judgment. Normally, an agency rule would be arbitrary and capricious if the agency has relied on factors which Congress has not intended it to consider, entirely failed to consider an important aspect of the problem, offered an explanation for its decision that runs counter to the evidence before the agency, or is so implausible that it could not be ascribed to a difference in view or the product of agency expertise.[11]

In other words, "[the rule must be] the product of reasoned decisionmaking."[12]

Today, arbitrary and capricious review is also known as "hard look" review. Originally, "hard-look review" focused on the competency of the agency's review of the record before it, not the

---

[8]   *Id.* at 416 (*quoting* APA § 706(A)(2)).

[9]   *Id.*

[10]   463 U.S. 29 (1983).

[11]   *Id.* at 43 (citations omitted).

[12]   *Id.* at 52.

appellate court's review of the agency's decision. As Judge Leventhal explained, hard-look review meant that a court would overturn agency decisions "if the court [became] aware . . . that the agency ha[d] not really taken a 'hard look' at the salient problems and ha[d] not genuinely engaged in reasoned decisionmaking."[13] Today, as a result of *Overton Park* and *State Farm*, "hard-look review" requires that a court ensure not only that the agency took a hard look at the problem but requires that the court itself take a hard look at the agency's resolution of that problem.

  3.   Arbitrary & Capricious Review v. Substantial Evidence Review

Both the substantial evidence and the arbitrary and capricious standards are framed in terms of the reasonableness of the agency's reasoning process. Moreover, arbitrary and capricious review has become less deferential. Hence, it is unclear whether these two standards reflect different levels of deference. Indeed, while a circuit judge, former Justice Scalia claimed that the two standards were essentially identical because "it is impossible to conceive of a non-arbitrary factual judgment supported only by evidence that is not substantial in the APA sense."[14] While the Supreme Court has never clearly addressed whether the two standards are different, the Court applied arbitrary and capricious review in *State Farm* even though the relevant statute expressly provided that the agency's determination had to be supported by "[s]ubstantial evidence on the record considered as a whole."[15] Some scholars suggest that this choice shows that the Court does not believe that these standards differ at all.

Other scholars argue that the standards are different; substantial evidence requires the court to conduct a slightly more searching inquiry. There is support to this argument; after all, Congress specifically identified two different standards in the APA. Moreover, Congress sometimes requires the substantial evidence standard in a statute when the arbitrary and capricious standard would be the default under the APA. In sum, we do not yet know whether the two standards truly reflect different intensity standards, but we do know the two standards are described differently. Be sure you use the correct description.

---

  [13]   Greater Boston Television v. FCC, 444 F.2d 841, 851 (D. C. Cir. 1970).

  [14]   Association of Data Processing Serv. Orgs. v. Board of Governors of Fed. Reserve Sys., 745 F.2d 677, 683 (D.C. Cir. 1984).

  [15]   *State Farm,* 463 U.S. at 44 (quoting S. Rep. No. 1301, 89th Cong., 2d Sess., 8 (1966); H. R. Rep. No. 1776, 89th Cong., 2d Sess., 21 (1966)).

C.   Defining Questions of Law & Mixed Questions

1.   Questions of Law

Assuming the issue to be resolved is not a question of fact or a question of policy, then it must be either a question of law or a mixed question. A statement of law is an assertion about legal effect that can be advanced with no knowledge of the facts in a particular case. Thus, a pure question of law is one in which the resolution of the question does not require any knowledge of the facts.

Let's return to our non-agency example, a car accident. During the investigation, the accident investigator noted that the speed limit was 30 mph on the road where the accident took place. This finding would be a finding of law. The facts are irrelevant.

Now, let's return to agencies. Agencies often resolve question of law, such as determining what language in a statute or regulation means. Assume that an agency must interpret its enabling statute to determine the boundaries of the authority Congress delegated to it. For example, the Food and Drug Administration had to determine whether tobacco was a "drug" or "drug delivery device," while the Treasure Department had to determine whether health care exchanges "established by the federal government" can also be established by a state (true story). In both of these situations, the question to be answered was one of law. Facts were irrelevant.

In a moment, we will focus on the standards of review that courts apply when agencies resolve pure questions of law (you will not be surprised to learn that there is more than one standard). But we must first cover another type of question that agencies resolve, questions of law application, or a mixed question of law and fact.

2.   Mixed Questions/Questions of Law Application

Mixed questions of law and fact, or application questions, occur during adjudication. Let's once again return to our car accident example. Assume the investigator concluded that the defendant must have exceeded the speed limit because the skid marks were unusually long. Such a question involves applying the relevant law (the speed limit) to the specific facts in a particular case (the unusually long skid marks) to reach a conclusion (the defendant was speeding). This question is a mixed question of law and fact.

Let's turn back to the world of agencies. During adjudications, agencies must determine whether a particular law applies to a given set of the facts. For example, in one case, an agency had to determine whether people who deliver newspapers were employees of a particular newspaper or were independent contractors.[16] In another case, an agency had to decide whether the refusal of an employer to bargain with its employees constituted an unfair labor practice. These questions were mixed questions: the agency had to consider both the facts and the law to resolve the question.

D. Standards of Review for Mixed Questions & Pure Questions of Law

1. Mixed Questions of Law & Fact

The appropriate standard applicable to mixed questions of law and fact is currently unclear. Some courts accept an agency's resolution of a mixed question if the resolution has "warrant in the record" and "a reasonable basis in the law."[17] Some courts treat the mixed question as a pure question of law, while others treat mixed questions as ones of fact.[18] Finally, some courts break the mixed question into its component parts: part law and part fact. To the extent the courts treat the question as one of fact, the standards of review from the preceding section apply. To the extent the courts treat the question as a pure question of law, the standards of review discussed below apply.

2. Questions of Law

When an agency interprets a statute or regulation during a rulemaking or adjudication, the agency has resolved a pure question of law. The Supreme Court has identified at least three standards of review that courts apply to review the agency's interpretation. The appropriate standard depends on the law the agency interpreted—a statute or regulation—and the process the agency used to make its interpretation—formal, informal, publication. We will start with agency interpretations of statutes.

a.   Agency Interpretation of Statutes

The Court has developed two standards of review for courts to use when reviewing agency interpretations of statutes. These two standards are known as *Chevron* and *Skidmore* analysis based on the cases in which the Court delineated the standard.

Chevron analysis applies when agencies use "force of law" procedures, while *Skidmore* analysis applies when agencies do not use "force of law" procedures. An agency uses "force of law"

---

[16]   *See, e.g.*, NLRB v. Hearst Publ'n, Inc., 322 U.S. 111 (1944).

[17]   *Id.* at 131.

[18]   *See, e.g.*, *O'Leary*, 340 U.S. at 507 (treating as a question of fact the issue of whether the death of a federal worker "arose out of and in the course of employment.").

procedures when "Congress . . . delegated legislative power to the agency and . . . the agency . . . exercise[d] that power in promulgating the rule."[19] In short, when an agency acts more deliberately and formally, the agency acts with "force of law."

For example, formal adjudication and notice-and-comment rulemaking are "force of law" procedures, while "opinion letters . . . policy statements, agency manuals, and enforcement guidelines . . . lack the force of law."[20]

Skidmore analysis is less deferential. We will start there.

i.   Skidmore

When agencies interpret statutes without using "force of law" procedures—for example, in a guidance document or during an informal adjudication—a court will apply *Skidmore* analysis to determine whether to defer to the agency's interpretation. To determine whether to defer, the court will consider "the thoroughness evident in [the agency's] consideration, the validity of its reasoning, its consistency with earlier or later pronouncements, and all those factors which give it power to persuade, if lacking power to control."[21] In short, an agency earns judicial deference under *Skidmore* by carefully, thoroughly, and consistently interpreting statutory language.

ii.   Chevron

In contrast, an agency earns judicial deference under *Chevron v. National Resources Defense Council, Inc.*,[22] simply because it is an agency that used force of law procedures. The Court described *Chevron* analysis as having two distinct steps. These two steps have been dubbed the "*Chevron* two-step." Pursuant to *Chevron*'s first step, a reviewing court should determine "whether Congress has directly spoken to the precise question at issue."[23] In other words, the court should determine whether congressional intent about the meaning of the language in the statute is clear. In doing so, a court must use the "traditional tools of statutory construction"; step one is not a simple search for textual clarity.[24]

At step one, courts do not defer to agency interpretations at all. Rather, "[t]he judiciary is the final authority on issues of statutory

---

[19]   American Mining Cong. v. Mine Safety & Health Admin., 995 F.2d 1106, 1109 (D.C. Cir. 1993) (defining "force of law").

[20]   Christensen v. Harris Cty., 529 U.S. 576, 587 (2000).

[21]   Skidmore v. Swift, 323 U.S. 134, 140 (1944).

[22]   467 U.S. 837 (1984).

[23]   *Id.* at 842–43.

[24]   *Id.* at 843 n.9.

construction . . . ."[25] While a court does not *defer* to an agency's interpretation at step one, the court will still affirm the agency's interpretation at this step if the agency's interpretation is consistent with congressional intent.

Assuming Congress's intent is not clear at step one, then, under step two, a court must accept any "permissible," or "reasonable," agency interpretation, even if the court believes a different policy choice would be better.[26] At step two, courts defer to agency interpretations that are within a range of possible statutory meanings. Courts understand that more than one interpretation is possible; the court must defer if the agency's interpretation is reasonable even if it is not the best interpretation. Deferring at step two is known as *Chevron* deference. Step two is supposed to be very differential to agencies, although it is becoming less so. When applying *Chevron*'s second step, the court defers to an agency's reasonable interpretation, but only if the agency has offered a reasoned explanation for why it chose that interpretation.[27] In other words, an agency must not act arbitrarily and capriciously in reaching an interpretation and that interpretation must be a reasonable one (process and outcome both matter).

The Supreme Court justified deferring to reasonable agency interpretations for three reasons. First, agency personnel are experts in their field while judges are not.[28] Second, Congress cannot legislate every detail in a comprehensive regulatory scheme; thus, gaps and ambiguities are inevitable. By leaving these gaps and ambiguities, Congress impliedly delegated authority to the agency to resolve them.[29] Third, administrative officials, unlike federal judges, have a political constituency to which they are accountable.[30]

Note that agencies have two bites at the apple: (1) their interpretation can control at step one if it is consistent with congressional intent, or (2) their interpretation can control at step two if Congress had no intended meaning, the agency's process for reaching a meaning is not arbitrary and capricious, and if the agency's interpretation is reasonable.

Skidmore analysis and *Chevron* analysis are the two standards of review courts apply when there are no pre-existing judicial

---

[25] *Id.* at 843.

[26] *Id.*

[27] *See* Encino Motorcars, LLC v. Navarro, 136 S. Ct. 2117, 2125 (2016).

[28] *Skidmore*, 323 U.S. at 865.

[29] *Id.* at 843–44.

[30] *Id.* at 866.

interpretations of that same statute. What if a court has already interpreted the statute and the agency wishes to interpret the statute differently? If the agency uses non-legislative procedures to interpret the statute differently from a court, then the standard of review is likely *Skidmore* analysis, although the Supreme Court has never made the appropriate standard clear. Given that *Skidmore* is a lower level of deference that considers the consistency of the agency's interpretation over time, it is likely the agency's interpretation would not survive *Skidmore* analysis. But what if the agency uses force of law procedures, when *Chevron* analysis would typically apply? In such a situation, *National Cable & Telecommunications Ass'n. v. Brand X Internet Services* (*Brand X*) applies.[31]

iii.   Brand X

When a court interprets language in a statute before an agency interprets the same language, the agency must interpret the language identically only if the court had reasoned that the statute was clear under *Chevron's* first step.[32] If the court held that congressional intent was not clear, then the court has just offered one interpretation of the statute, and the agency remains free to adopt another interpretation of that statute so long as its interpretation is reasonable and its process is not arbitrary and capricious.

b.   Agency Interpretations of Regulations

Chevron analysis is applicable only when an agency interprets a specific type of legal text: a statute. *Chevron* does not apply when agencies interpret the Federal Constitution, court opinions, and legal instruments such as contracts. Similarly, *Chevron* does not apply when agencies interpret other agencies' regulations. Indeed, in these situations, courts do not defer at all.

More importantly, when an agency interprets its own regulation, neither *Chevron* nor *Skidmore* apply. Instead, in 1945, the Supreme Court held that an agency's interpretation of its own regulation has "controlling weight unless it is plainly erroneous or inconsistent with the regulation."[33] In 1997, after the Court had decided *Chevron*, the Court confirmed that the plainly erroneous" deference standard survived *Chevron*;[34] hence, deference to agency's

---

[31]   545 U.S. 967, 982 (2005).

[32]   *Id.* at 982.

[33]   Bowles v. Seminole Rock & Sand Co., 325 U.S. 410, 414 (1945).

[34]   Auer v. Robbins, 519 U.S. 452, 461–63 (1997).

interpretations of their own regulations is called either *Seminole Rock* (the 1945 case) or *Auer* (the 1997 case) deference.

There is at least one limit on when an agency will receive *Auer* deference. When an agency does little more than parrot statutory language in one regulation, then "interprets" that language in a second regulation, the agency is not entitled to *Auer* deference. In such a case, the agency is merely parroting the statute (meaning the agency simply copies the language Congress used). Hence, the agency will not receive *Auer* deference because the agency is interpreting Congress's language, not its own.[35] Thus, *Chevron* or *Skidmore* analysis is appropriate.

        STANDARD CHECKLIST

A. **Type of Finding/Question:**

    1. Is the court reviewing a finding of fact or policy?

        a. **No**—If no, then <u>proceed to A.2. below</u>.

        b. **Yes**—If yes, then ask whether the agency made its finding as a part of a formal adjudication or a formal rulemaking.

            i. **Yes**—If yes, then the reviewing court will review the agency's finding using the substantial evidence standard. <u>Proceed to B.1. below</u>.

            ii. **No**—If no, then the reviewing court will review the agency's finding using the arbitrary and capricious standard. <u>Proceed to B.2. below</u>.

    2. Is the court reviewing a finding of law?

        a. **No**—If no, then <u>proceed to A.3. below</u>.

        b. **Yes**—If yes, then ask the following:

            i. Is the agency interpreting language in a constitution or contract?

                (a). Yes—If yes, then the reviewing court will review the agency's interpretation *de novo*. <u>Stop here</u>.

                (b). No—If no, then <u>proceed to A.2.b.ii</u>.

---

[35] Gonzales v. Oregon, 546 U.S. 243, 257 (2006) (refusing also to apply *Chevron* analysis because the agency's regulation was not a legislative rule).

    ii. Is the agency interpreting language in its own regulation?

        (a). Yes—If yes, then *Auer* deference may apply. Proceed to B.5. below.

        (b). No—If no, then proceed to A.2.b.iii.

    iii. Is the agency interpreting language in a statute that the agency administers?

        (a). Yes—If yes, then ask whether the agency made its finding as a part of a formal adjudication, a formal rulemaking, or a notice-and-comment rulemaking.

            – **Yes**—If yes, then the reviewing court will review the agency's finding using *Chevron* analysis. Proceed to B.4. below.

            – **No**—If no, then the reviewing court will review the agency's finding using *Skidmore* analysis. Proceed to B.3. below.

        (b). No—If no, then the reviewing court will review the agency's interpretation of a statute it does not administer *de novo*. Stop here.

3. Is the court reviewing a mixed finding of law/law application?

    a. **No**—If no, then return to A.1. You have made an error.

    b. **Yes**—If yes, then follow the analysis for findings of fact (A.1.) for that portion of the finding and follow the analysis for findings of law (A.2.) for that portion of the finding.

B. **Standards of Review:** (After identifying the standard of review, apply it).

1. If the substantial evidence standard of review applies, then ask whether the evidence in the record would allow a reasonable person to make the same finding that the agency made.

    a. **No**—If no, then the court will reject the agency's finding. Stop here.

  b. **Yes**—If yes, then the court will uphold the agency's finding. <u>Stop here</u>. Substantial evidence is defined as such relevant evidence as a reasonable mind might accept as adequate to support a conclusion.

2. If the arbitrary and capricious standard of review applies, ask the following: was the agency's decision (1) based on a consideration of all the relevant factors, and (2) free of clear error? (Both elements must be satisfied).

  a. **No**—If no, then the court will reject the agency's finding. <u>Stop here</u>.

  b. **Yes**—If yes, then the court will uphold the agency's finding. <u>Stop here</u>. A non-arbitrary and capricious decision is one that was based on a consideration of all the relevant factors and has no clear errors of judgment.

3. If *Skidmore* analysis applies, then balance the following three factors: (1) the thoroughness evident in the agency's consideration of the issue, (2) the validity of the agency's reasoning for its interpretation, and (3) the consistency of the agency's interpretation over time. Does the balancing of these factors support the agency's finding?

  a. **No**—If no, then the court will reject the agency's interpretation. <u>Stop here</u>.

  b. **Yes**—If yes, then the court will uphold the agency's interpretation because the agency was persuasive. <u>Stop here</u>.

4. If *Chevron* analysis applies, then ask the following questions:

  a. Has a court already interpreted the same language differently from the agency?

    i. **No**—If no, <u>Proceed to 4.b. below</u>. Because there is no prior court interpretation, the agency is not bound by one.

    ii. **Yes**—If yes, then ask whether the prior court reached its interpretation at *Chevron*'s first step?

      (a). No—If no, then the prior court reached its interpretation based on its conclusion of what was the best interpretation and not based on what Congress demanded. The agency is free to reach a different interpretation so long as that interpretation is reasonable under *Chevron*'s second step. Proceed to 4.c.

   (b). Yes—If yes, the prior judicial interpretation controls because Congress has spoken, and the court will reject any agency interpretation that is not consistent with the prior judicial interpretation. Stop here.

b. Using the traditional tools of statutory interpretation, apply *Chevron*'s first step by asking whether Congress has spoken directly to the precise issue before the court (congressional intent)?

   i.   No—If no, Proceed to 4.c. If Congress does not have a specific intent as to the language at issue, the Congress impliedly delegated resolution of the statute's meaning to the agency.

   ii.   Yes—If yes, ask whether the agency's interpretation is consistent with congressional intent.

   (a). No—If no, then the agency's interpretation is invalid because it conflicts with Congressional intent. Stop here. (You may wish to argue in the alternative and reach *Chevron*'s second step).

   (b). Yes—If yes, then the agency's interpretation is valid because it is consistent with congressional intent. Stop here. (You may wish to argue in the alternative and reach *Chevron*'s second step).

c. If Congress has not directly spoken to the precise issue before the court, apply *Chevron*'s second step by asking whether the agency has offered a reasoned explanation for why it chose that interpretation and whether the interpretation is reasonable?

   i.   No—If no, then the agency's interpretation is invalid because is unreasonable or the process was arbitrary and capricious. Stop here.

   ii.   Yes—If yes, then the agency's interpretation is valid. Stop here.

5. If *Auer* analysis applies, then ask the following questions:

    a. Did the agency simply parrot the statutory language in its first regulation and then interpret the parroting language in its second regulation?

        i. **No**—If no, proceed to B.5.b.

        ii. **Yes**—If yes, the agency's interpretation is not entitled to *Auer* analysis. If the agency's second regulation is legislative, then *Chevron* analysis applies. Return to B.4. above. If the agency's second regulation is non-legislative, then *Skidmore* analysis applies. Return to B.3. above.

    b. Is the agency's interpretation plainly erroneous or inconsistent with the regulation it is interpreting?

        i. **No**—If no, then the agency's interpretation of its own regulation is valid. Stop here.

        ii. **Yes**—If yes, then the agency's interpretation of its own regulation is invalid. Stop here.

ILLUSTRATIVE PROBLEMS

■ PROBLEM 7.1 ■

Assume that the Department of Education (DOE) administers a program known as "Children Are Exceptional" (CARE). CARE implements the president's policy of "decreasing drug use, teenage pregnancy, and domestic violence through education." To this end, under CARE, the DOE provides federal funds to schools that meet certain criteria. The enabling statute authorizes DOE to promulgate rules "after hearing." Assume, the DOE published a notice of proposed rulemaking (NPRM) and invited comments on how DOE could best meet the program's objectives.

To decrease teenage pregnancy, the DOE proposed in its NPRM that public school sex education classes address abstinence-only options. The American Academy of Pediatrics commented that there were no studies that supported the proposition that abstinence-only education decreased teenage pregnancy. Similarly, the American Public Health Association cited multiple studies finding that comprehensive sex education programs that include a discussion of abstinence are more effective in decreasing teenage pregnancy than abstinence-only education programs. And the American Medical Association sent the DOE a copy of the numerous studies conducted, none of which supported the agency's proposed rule. A group called Mom's Against Teenagers Having Sex wrote to support the proposed rule, arguing that teens should not have sex.

Assume that the DOE promulgates the final rule and makes no changes after the notice-and-comment period has ended. If the American Medical Association files suit, what standard of review should the reviewing court apply and how will the court likely rule?

Analysis

The first issue here is what standard of review the court will apply to the DOE's decision to require abstinence only education, which was made during a notice-and-comment rulemaking. Using the checklist above (A.1.), you should first conclude that this decision (or finding) is a policy decision. Next, because the agency made its decision as a part of a notice-and-comment rulemaking, the reviewing court will review the agency's finding using the arbitrary and capricious standard of review in APA § 706(2)(A).

The second issue here is how a court would rule after applying the standard identified above. A court applying arbitrary and capricious review should ask the following questions: (1) whether the agency's decision was based on a consideration of all the relevant factors (as identified in the statute), and (2) whether the judgment was free of clear error. Further, for policy decisions, reviewing courts will look to see whether there was a rational connection between the facts in the record and the policy decision.[36]

Here, the statute is not provided, so we do not know whether the agency was directed to consider specific factors. However, the overwhelming factual evidence in the record does not support the DOE's policy finding, including the American Academy of Pediatrics' comment that no studies supported the proposition that abstinence-only education decreased teenage pregnancy; the studies cited by the American Public Health Association, finding that comprehensive sex education programs that include a discussion of abstinence are more effective in decreasing teenage pregnancy than abstinence-only education programs; and the studies sent by the American Medical Association, none of which supported the agency's proposed rule. The only evidentiary support for the agency's position came from the views of Mom's Against Teenagers Having Sex. Thus, the decision does not appear to be free or error. Moreover, there was no rational connection between the facts in the record and the agency's policy decision. Hence, the court would likely find the DOE's policy decision to be arbitrary and capricious.

---

[36] Motor Vehicle Manuf. Ass'n v. State Farm Mut. Auto. Ins. Co., 463 U.S. 29, 42–43 (1983).

■ **PROBLEM 7.2** ■

The Social Security Act directs the Social Security Administration (SSA) to pay disability insurance benefits to individual with disabilities. The Act defines an individual with a disability as follows:

> An individual shall be determined to be under a disability only if his physical or mental impairment or impairments are of such severity that he is not only unable to do his previous work but cannot, considering his age, education, and work experience, engage in any other kind of substantial gainful work *which exists in the national economy.*

The SSA promulgated a rule interpreting the modifying phrase "which exists in the national economy" to modify only the phrase "any other kind of substantial gainful work." The SSA applied the rule of last antecedent to reach this interpretation. Under SSA's interpretation, someone who applies for disability benefits must prove both (1) that she could not preform the previous job because of her physical or mental impairment, and (2) that she could not perform any other substantial gainful work that exists in the national economy because of her physical or mental impairment. Further, it is irrelevant whether the applicant's prior job even exists in the national economy when she applies because the SSA rejected an interpretation that would have applied the modifier to both the phrase "his previous work" and the phrase "any other kind of substantial gainful work." Had the SSA adopted this alternate interpretation, someone who applies for disability benefits would need to prove (1) that she could not perform the previous job because it no longer exists in the national economy (her physical or mental impairment would not be relevant), and (2) that she could not perform any other substantial gainful work that exists in the national economy because of her physical or mental impairment.

Ellen is an individual who has heart disease and cervical and lumbar radiculopathy. She worked as an elevator operator. Her job was eliminated, so she was let go. Elevator operator jobs no longer exist in the national economy. She applied for disability benefits, alleging that she was disabled. An Administrative Law Judge (ALJ) applied the SSA's definition and found that because Ellen's impairments did not prevent her from performing her prior job as an elevator operator she was not disabled, even though that job no longer existed anywhere.

On appeal, the SSA's Appeal Council denied Ellen's request for review. Assume that Ellen appeals the SSA's decision in federal court. What standard of review will a court apply to the SSA's interpretation of the Social Security Act if the agency's interpretation was made during notice-and-comment rulemaking? Instead, what if the interpretation were made as an interpretive rule that did not go through notice-and-comment rulemaking (or formal rulemaking)? Assume that there is no relevant legislative history, the statute is remedial, and its purpose is to aid the disabled.

Analysis

The issue in this problem is to identify and apply the appropriate standard of review. First, let's identify the appropriate standard of review. Using the checklist above (A.1.), you should determine that the court is not reviewing a finding of fact or policy; rather, the court is reviewing an agency's interpretation of language in a statute, specifically the SSA's interpretation of language in the Social Security Act. Thus, the court would be reviewing an agency's finding of law. Because the SSA made that interpretation as part of a notice-and-comment rulemaking, *Chevron* analysis applies.

Second, let's apply that standard of review to the problem. To determine whether a court would defer to the SSA's interpretation using *Chevron* analysis, you must first, identify the language in the statute that the agency interpreted and the agency's interpretation of that language. Here, the question tells you that the language the SSA interpreted in the statute is "which exists in the national economy." Further, the question explains that the SSA interpreted that language to modify only "any other kind of substantial gainful work" and not that phrase "his previous work."

Before applying *Chevron*'s two-step analysis, you should ask whether a court has already interpreted the same language. In this case, the answer is no, so you may proceed to *Chevron*'s two-step analysis. Apply step one first, using the traditional tools of statutory interpretation. At step one, you need to determine whether Congress has spoken directly to the precise issue before the court. In this case, the text of the Social Security Act and the doctrine of last antecedent both suggest that Congress intended the modifier to apply only to the second phrase, which is consistent with the SSA's interpretation. Further, there is no legislative history pointing in either direction.

However, the Social Security Act is a remedial statute that should be interpreted to further its remedial purpose. The remedial purpose is to help individuals with disabilities who cannot otherwise find work. The SSA's interpretation does not further that remedial purpose. Moreover, the SSA's interpretation would be absurd. Under the SSA's interpretation, Ellen is not disabled because she could perform her prior job, even though that job no longer exists anywhere and she cannot perform any jobs that do exist. In short, she has no way to make a living; yet, she is considered non-disabled.

Arguably, the text and the doctrine of last antecedent conflict with the remedial canon, the purpose of the statute, and the absurdity doctrine. If a court were to find that text and linguistic canons controlled, then the SSA's interpretation is consistent with congressional intent and that interpretation is valid. If, instead, the court were to conclude that Congress did not directly speak to this issue because the traditional tools point in opposite directions, then Congress impliedly delegated resolution of this ambiguity to the SSA.

Assuming the court determined that Congress had not directly spoken to the precise issue before the court, then the court would apply *Chevron*'s second step to determine whether the SSA offered a reasoned explanation for why it chose that interpretation and whether the interpretation was reasonable. Here, the SSA used the traditional tools of statutory interpretation to interpret the statute consistently with the text and the doctrine of last antecedent. Moreover the interpretation is within the range of reasonableness, even if it is not the best interpretation.[37]

If instead, the interpretation were made as an interpretive rule that did not go through notice-and-comment rulemaking, then a court would review the SSA's finding using *Skidmore* analysis. Under *Skidmore* analysis, the court would balance the following three factors: (1) the thoroughness evident in the agency's consideration of the issue, (2) the validity of the agency's reasoning for its interpretation, and (3) the consistency of the agency's interpretation over time. In this case, the facts are silent regarding consistency and thoroughness. However, the SSA offered valid reasons, based on statutory interpretation canons, for interpreting the language as it did. Likely, the court would defer to the agency's interpretation as persuasive.

POINTS TO REMEMBER

- After determining that a court will review an agency's action (reviewability from Chapter 6), you need to determine the appropriate standard of review.

---

[37]   *See* Barnhart v. Thomas, 540 U.S. 20 (2003) (giving deference to the SSA's interpretation).

- The appropriate standard of review depends on a number of factors, including the type of finding/issue and the formality of the process the agency used to make the finding.

- Courts review agency findings of fact and policy decisions made during formal rulemaking and formal adjudication using the substantial evidence standard. A court applying that standard would determine whether the agency relied on "such relevant evidence as a reasonable mind might accept as adequate to support a conclusion."

- Courts review agency findings of fact and policy decisions made during informal rulemaking, non-legislative rulemaking, and informal adjudication using the arbitrary and capricious standard. A court applying that standard would determine "whether the decision was based on a consideration of the relevant factors and whether there has been a clear error of judgment." Additionally, for policy decisions, reviewing courts will look to see whether there was a rational connection between the facts in the record and the policy decision made.

- Courts review agency interpretations of statutory language, which were made during formal rulemaking, formal adjudication, and notice-and-comment rulemaking using *Chevron* analysis. A court applying *Chevron* analysis would determine first whether Congress has spoken to the precise issue before the court, using the traditional tools of statutory interpretation. If Congress has not spoken, then the court would evaluate whether the agency offered a reasoned explanation for why it chose that interpretation and whether the interpretation was reasonable.

- Courts review agency interpretations of statutory language made during informal adjudication and non-legislative rulemaking using *Skidmore* analysis. A court applying that standard would examine "the thoroughness evident in [the agency's] consideration, the validity of its reasoning, its consistency with earlier or later pronouncements, and all those factors which give it power to persuade, if lacking power to control."

- Courts review agency interpretations of language in the agency's own regulations using *Auer* analysis. A court applying *Auer* analysis would reject an agency's interpretation only if it were plainly wrong or inconsistent with the regulation the agency is interpreting.

CHAPTER 8

The Big Picture

 THE ENTIRE CHECKLIST

In this chapter, all of the checklists from the prior chapters have been joined in one, large checklist. After the checklist, a long exam question with various subparts is included to test your understanding of the topic and ability to use the checklist to answer a previously used exam question. Finally, brief answers to the subparts are included to guide your analysis, not to provide you with canned answers—trust me when I say that canned answers are always a bad way to write an exam answer.

Further, the answers raise and dismiss non-issues quickly to show you how to work through the checklist, not because non-issues should be addressed. Some professors prefer that students do not waste time addressing non-issues, while others will give students points for raising and dismissing them quickly. You would do well to figure out which type of professor you have. In addition, you will need to augment these brief answers substantially if you wish to do well on your exam. The answers do not include cases, full explanations, or complete analysis and counter-analysis. However, the sample answers provide you with a plan of attack: a way to use the checklist to be sure that you do not miss important issues or apply the wrong analysis. The rest is up to you!

I. IS THERE AGENCY ACTION? (CHAPTER 1)

A. *Agency* Action—Is the actor an authority of the United States government, such as an administration, commission, corporation, board, department, division, or agency?

    1. **No**—If no, the actor is not an agency, and the APA does not apply. The president, Congress, a federal court, a state or territorial government, a military commission or court

martial, and specifically exempted authorities under APA §§ 551(1)(A)–(H) are not agencies. Stop here.

2. **Yes**—If yes, the actor is a federal agency, and administrative law applies. Proceed to I.B. below.

B. Agency *Action*—Did the agency act, fail to act, or unreasonably delay acting?

1. **No**—If the agency did not act and was not required to act or if the agency did not unreasonably delay acting, then the APA does not apply. Stop here.

2. **Yes**—If the agency acted or failed to act when legally required, the APA applies. Proceed to I.C. below. If the agency unreasonably delayed acting, then the APA applies. If the agency acted or failed to act when legally required, the APA applies. Proceed to I.C. below. If the agency unreasonably delayed acting, then the APA applies. To determine whether the agency's delay was reasonable, a reviewing court will apply the TRAC factors. *Telecommunications Research & Action Ctr. v. FCC*, 750 F.2d 70, 76 (D.C. Cir. 1984) (identifying the following factors: whether the applicable statute contains a timetable, whether delay will impact human welfare, how forcing decision would affect higher agency priorities, and how all the interests are affected).

C. Agency *Action*—How did the agency act?

1. **Rulemaking**—Did the agency promulgate a general rule with future application?

    a. **No**—If no, the agency may have acted using adjudicatory powers. Proceed to I.C.2. below.

    b. **Yes**—If yes, the agency acted via rulemaking, and the APA applies. Proceed to II below.

2. **Adjudication**—Did the agency issue an order that applies to specific parties and their past actions?

    a. **No**—If no, the agency may have acted using informational powers. Proceed to I.C.3. below.

    b. **Yes**—If yes, the agency acted using adjudication, and the APA applies. Ask whether the agency legitimately choose to use adjudication rather than rulemaking to make a new policy?

        i. **No**—If a party was substantially penalized for abiding by prior policy, then the agency's choice is invalid, and any order should be set aside. *NLRB v. Bell Aerospace Co. Div. of Textron Inc.*, 416 U.S. 267 (1974). Stop here.

    ii. **Yes**—If yes, the agency's choice is valid. Proceed to II below.

3. Information Gathering—Did the agency seek information through an inspection, with a request for information, or by subpoena?

    a. **No**—If no, you have reached a wrong answer at some point in your analysis. Start over.

    b. **Yes**—If yes, the agency acted using executive powers and administrative law applies, but not the APA. Proceed to II below.

II. DID THE AGENCY HAVE AUTHORITY TO ACT? (CHAPTER 2)

A. *Statutory Authority*—Does the Agency have *statutory* authority to act?

1. Does the enabling or another statute authorize the agency to conduct rulemaking, adjudication, or investigation, as applicable?

    a. **No**—If no, the agency has no legal authority to act. Stop here. *Caveat*: Note that an agency does not need statutory authority to announce what its policy is or how it interprets a statute or regulation because such actions do not make law.

    b. **Yes**—If yes, proceed to II.A.2. below.

2. Did the agency comply with all additional requirements in the enabling statute, other relevant statutes, and relevant executive orders (*e.g.*, the Regulatory Flexibility Act and E.O. 12,866)?

    a. **No**—If no, the agency must go back and follow these procedures. Stop here.

    b. **Yes**—If yes, proceed to II.B. below.

B. *Constitutional Authority*—Is the agency's structure constitutional? (Warning, the law in this area is far from settled and does not lend itself to a simple checklist answer).

1. **Appointment**—Is the relevant actor a principal officer (typically heads of agencies), an inferior officer (those working closely with the heads of agencies), or an employee? Officers hold "continuing" positions established by law and exercise "significant authority." Inferior officers have supervisors.

a.   **Principal Officer**—If the officer is a principal officer, does the enabling statute provide that the president will appoint and the Senate must confirm?

    i.   **No**—If no, the statute is unconstitutional, and the officer has no authority to act. <u>Stop here.</u>

    ii. **Yes**—If yes, the officer is constitutionally appointed under U.S. CONST. art. II § 2 cl. 2. <u>Proceed to II.B.2. below.</u>

b.   **Inferior Officer**—If the officer is an inferior officer, does the enabling statutory vest the appointment power in the president, the courts of law, or in the head of a department?

    i.   **No**—If no, the statute is unconstitutional, and the officer has no authority to act. <u>Stop here.</u>

    ii. **Yes**—If yes, the officer is constitutionally appointed under U.S. CONST. art. II § 2 cl. 2. <u>Proceed to II.B.2. below.</u>

c.   **Employee**—If the officer is an employee, there are no constitutional requirements relating to appointment. Congress can limit the appointment and removal of employees as it wishes. <u>Proceed to II.B.2. below.</u>

2.   **Removal**—Is there any limit on the president's power to remove the relevant actor, such as a for-cause restriction?

a.   **No**—If no, then the actor is constitutionally removable under the Constitution because there are no limits on the president's power to remove. <u>Proceed to II.C. below.</u>

b.   **Yes**—If yes, then ask whether the relevant actor is a principal officer, an inferior officer, or an employee? (See above for definitions).

    i.   **Principal Officer**—If the officer is a principal officer, ask whether the officer performs purely executive acts.

        (a). Executive Acts—If the officer performs purely executive acts, then any restriction is likely unconstitutional under *Myers*. <u>Stop here.</u>

(b). Quasi-Legislative/Adjudicatory Acts—If the officer performs quasi-legislative/adjudicator acts, then the restriction is likely unconstitutional under *Humphrey's Executor*. Proceed to II.C. below.

ii. **Inferior Officer**—If the officer is an inferior officer, then ask whether the president can perform her or his constitutional duty to ensure that the laws are faithfully executed with the removal restriction in place. Generally, single for-cause removal restrictions are constitutional, while dual for-cause removal restrictions are unconstitutional.

    (a). No—If no, then any restriction is likely unconstitutional under *Free Enterprise*. Stop here.

    (b). Yes—If yes, then any restriction is likely constitutional under *Free Enterprise*. Proceed to II.C. below.

iii. **Employee**—If the officer is an employee, then the actor is constitutionally removable under the Constitution. Congress can limit the appointment and removal of employees as it wishes. Proceed to II.C. below.

C. *Constitutional Authority*—Does the agency have *constitutional* authority to act?

1. **For Rulemaking**—Did Congress provide an *intelligible principle* to guide the agency's decisionmaking? Examples of intelligible principles include "requisite to protect the public health," "necessary to avoid an imminent hazard to the public safety," "adequately assures . . . that no employee will suffer any impairment of health," and "[not] unduly or unnecessarily complicate[d]."

   a. **No**—If no, which is unlikely, the statute is unconstitutional and the agency has no legal authority to act. Stop here.

   b. **Maybe**—If maybe, consider whether the court should apply the constitutional avoidance doctrine to avoid interpreting the statute in a way that would violate the delegation doctrine. If so, proceed to III below.

    c.   **Yes**—If yes, the statute is constitutional. <u>Proceed to III below</u>.

  2.   **For Adjudication**—Does the issue involve public rights, meaning an issue arising between the government and another, or private rights, meaning an issue arising between individuals and entities other than the government?

    a.   **Private Rights**—If the issue involves only private rights, then the delegation is likely unconstitutional. <u>Stop here</u>.

    b.   **Public Rights**—If the issue involves public rights, then the delegation is likely constitutional. <u>Proceed to IV below</u>.

  3.   **For Investigation**—<u>Proceed to V. below</u>.

III.   DID THE AGENCY FOLLOW APPROPRIATE RULEMAKING PROCEDURES? (CHAPTER 3)

A. **Initiating Rulemaking**—Who initiated rulemaking?

  1.   Did a citizen petition to issue, amend, or repeal a rule?

    a.   **No**—If no, then there is no agency action until the petition is granted, denied, or ignored. <u>Stop here</u>.

    b.   **Yes**—If yes, proceed to III.A.2. below.

  2.   Did the agency grant the petition and initiate rulemaking?

    a.   **No**—If the petition was not granted, then the agency either denied or delayed acting on the petition. <u>Proceed to III.A.3. below</u>.

    b.   **Yes**—If yes, then you will need to evaluate the agency's choice of rulemaking procedure. <u>Proceed to III.B. below</u>.

  3.   Did the agency delay acting on the petition?

    a.   **No**—If there is no delay at this time, then the agency must have denied the petition. <u>Proceed to A.4. below</u>.

    b.   **Yes**—If yes, then the agency's delay is subject to judicial review under TRAC's rule of reason test. Evaluate (1) whether Congress provided a timetable for the agency action; (2) whether the delay negatively affects human health and welfare; (3) whether expediting the delay would lead to negative effect on issues of higher priority for the agency; and (4) whether the nature and extent of other interests would be unduly prejudiced by the delay. Courts are very deferential of agency decisions to delay. <u>Stop here</u>.

4.   Did the agency deny the petition?

   a.   **No**—If no, then the agency must have either granted the petition or delayed acting on it. <u>Return to A.2. & A.3. above</u>.

   b.   **Yes**— If the petition was denied, then the denial is agency action subject to judicial review. <u>Proceed to the checklists in Chapters 6 and 7</u> to see whether judicial review is available and whether the agency's decision was valid. <u>Stop here</u>.

B.   **Choice of Rulemaking Procedure**—Did the agency use the appropriate procedure?

   1.   Did the agency use notice-and-comment rulemaking or publication rulemaking procedures when it was required to use formal rulemaking procedures?

      a.   Did the enabling statute include the phrase "on the record after a hearing" or similar words?

         i.   **No**—If no, then the agency could choose to use formal rulemaking procedures but was not required to do so under the APA unless the enabling statute otherwise specifically required formal procedures. The court will apply *Chevron* analysis to evaluate the agency's choice (see VII.B.4. below).

            (a). If the agency used publication rulemaking procedures, <u>proceed to III.B.2. below</u>.

            (b). If the agency used notice-and-comment rulemaking procedures, <u>proceed to III.C. below</u>.

         ii.   **Yes**—If yes, then the agency was required to use formal rulemaking procedures, and its decision not to is invalid. <u>Stop here</u>.

   2.   Did the agency use publication rulemaking procedures when it was required to use notice-and-comment rulemaking procedures?

      a.   Does the rule relate to (1) to military and foreign affairs; (2) to agency management and personnel, or

(3) to public property, loans, grants, benefits, and contracts?

    i.   **No**—If no, then the rule may still be exempt from notice-and-comment rulemaking procedures. <u>Proceed to III.B.2.b. below</u>.

    ii.   **Yes**—If yes, then the agency was not required to use notice-and-comment rulemaking procedures (unless the enabling statute expressly so provided). The rule is valid. <u>Proceed to III.C. below</u>.

b.   Did the agency have good cause to believe that notice would be impracticable, unnecessary, or contrary to the public interest?

    i.   **No**—If no, then the rule may still be exempt from notice-and-comment rulemaking procedures. <u>Proceed to III.B.2.c. below</u>.

    ii.   **Yes**—If yes, then the agency was not required to use notice-and-comment rulemaking procedures because it has "good cause" to skip those procedures (unless the enabling statute expressly so provided). The rule is valid. <u>Proceed to III.C. below</u>.

c.   Is the rule a procedural rule, which does not have a substantial impact on the rights of the people affected by it (or, if in D.C., does the rule encode a substantial value judgment)[1]?

    i.   **No**—If no, then the rule may still be exempt from notice-and-comment rulemaking procedures. <u>Proceed to III.B.2.d. below</u>.

    ii.   **Yes**—If yes, then the agency was not required to use notice-and-comment rulemaking procedures (unless the enabling statute expressly so provided). The rule is valid. <u>Proceed to III.C. below</u>.

d.   Does the rule *prospectively* advise the public and agency personnel on the way in which the agency plans to exercise *discretionary* power in the future?

---

[1]   The D.C. Circuit applies a different test. It examines whether the rule encodes a substantive value judgment and substantially alters the rights of the parties; if so, notice-and-comment procedures are necessary. JEM Broadcasting Co., Inc. v. FCC, 22 F.3d 320, 328 (D.C. Cir. 1994).

    i.   **No**—If no, then the rule likely imposes rights and obligations or restricts agency's ability to exercise its discretion (binding effects test). It is not a valid policy statement, exempt from notice-and-comment rulemaking; however, another exception to notice-and-comment rulemaking may apply. <u>Proceed to III.B.2.e. below</u>.

    ii. **Yes**—If yes, then the rule is a non-legislative rule, specifically a policy statement, for which the agency was not required to use notice-and-comment rulemaking (unless the enabling statute expressly so provided). The rule is valid. <u>Proceed to III.C. below</u>.

  e. Does the rule interpret language in an existing statute or regulation?

    i.   **No**—If no, then either you made a mistake or the rule is a legislative rule, and the agency was required to use notice-and-comment rulemaking procedures. The rule is invalid. <u>Stop here</u>.

    ii. **Yes**—If yes, then determine whether the agency intended to exercise legislative rulemaking authority. Determine whether the "intent to exercise" factors are present: (1) must the agency refer to an existing legislative rule to enforce the new rule; (2) is the new rule published in the Code of Federal Regulations; (3) did the agency invoke its legislative rulemaking authority to issue the new rule; or (4) is the new rule inconsistent with a prior legislative rule. Are any of the four "intent to exercise" factors are present?

      (a). **No**—If no, then the rule is a non-legislative, interpretive rule, for which the agency was not required to use notice-and-comment rulemaking (unless the enabling statute expressly so provided). The rule is valid. <u>Proceed to III.C. below</u>.

      (b). **Yes**—If yes, then the agency likely intended to use its legislative rulemaking authority and should not have used publication procedures. The rulemaking process was invalid. <u>Stop here</u>.

C. **Rulemaking Procedures**—Did the agency follow the appropriate procedures?

    1. Did the agency use publication procedures?

        a. **No**—If no, then the agency used either notice-and-comment rulemaking or formal rulemaking procedures (with hybrid procedures). <u>Proceed to III.C.2. below</u>.

        b. **Yes**—If yes, and the agency published the rule or provided personal notice to the relevant entity, the rule is valid. <u>Stop here</u>.

    2. Did the agency use notice-and-comment rulemaking procedures?

        a. Did the *notice* include the time, place, and nature of any public proceedings; the legal authority for the rule; and either the substance of the proposed rule or a description of the subjects and issues involved? Was the notice "sufficient to fairly apprise interested persons of the issues involved, so that they may present responsive data or argument"?[2]

            i. **No**—If no, then the notice was insufficient. <u>Stop here</u>.

            ii. **Yes**—If yes, then the notice was sufficient. <u>Proceed to III.C.2.b. below</u>.

        b. Did the agency engage in ex parte communications during the rulemaking process?

            i. **No**—If no, then <u>proceed to III.C.2.c below</u>. Generally, ex parte communications are not prohibited for notice-and-comment rulemaking.

            ii. **Yes**—If yes, ask whether the rulemaking proceeding involved "conflicting private claims to a valuable privilege," like a license. If so, the ex parte communications violated the Due Process Clause of the Fifth Amendment and the rulemaking is invalid. If not, <u>proceed to III.C.2.c. below</u>. Generally, ex parte communications are not prohibited for notice-and-comment rulemaking.

---

    [2] The D.C. Circuit also requires the notice contain all the scientific data and methodology on which the agency relied. Portland Cement Ass'n v. Ruckelshaus, 486 F.2d 375, 394 (D.C. Cir. 1973).

    c. Did the agency allow interested parties to submit "written data, views, or arguments" on the proposed rule?

        i. **No**—If no, then the comment process was insufficient, and the rule is invalid. Stop here.

        ii. **Yes**—If yes, then the comment opportunity was sufficient. Proceed to III.C.2.d below.

    d. Did the agency follow any hybrid procedures as required by the enabling statute, the agency's regulations, or other statutes? Note that a court cannot require additional procedures under *Vermont Yankee*.

        i. **No**—If no, then the rulemaking process was insufficient and the rule is invalid. Stop here.

        ii. **Yes** If yes, then the rulemaking process was valid. Proceed to III.C.2.e. below.

    e. Can the final rule be characterized as a "logical outgrowth" of the proposed rule, meaning that the final rule did not materially alter the issues involved in the rulemaking and the final rule did not substantially depart from the substance of the proposed rule (there were no surprise switcheroos)?

        i. **No**—If no, then the notice was insufficient. Stop here.

        ii. **Yes**—If yes, then the notice was sufficient, and the final rule was validly promulgated. Proceed to VI and VII below to see if the substance of the rule is valid and can be challenged in court.

  3. Did the agency use formal rulemaking procedures?

    a. **No**—If no, you have reached a wrong answer at some point in your analysis. Start over.

    b. **Yes**—If yes, then proceed to IV below to determine whether the agency correctly followed the formal rulemaking requirements.

IV. DID THE AGENCY FOLLOW APPROPRIATE ADJUDICATION PROCEDURES? (CHAPTER 4)

A. **Choice of Adjudication Procedure**—Was the agency required to use formal adjudication procedures because the enabling statute includes the phrase "on the record after a hearing" or similar words?

1. **No**—If no, then under *Chevron*'s two-step test the agency could proceed using informal procedures. <u>Proceed to C. below</u>.

2. **Yes**—If yes, then under *Chevron*'s two-step test the agency was required to use formal procedures. To determine whether the agency correctly followed formal procedures <u>proceed to B. below</u>. If the agency did not use formal procedures, its choice was invalid. <u>Stop here</u>.

B. **Formal Adjudication Procedures**—Did the agency follow appropriate procedures?

1. Did the agency notify "persons entitled to notice of an agency hearing" regarding when and where the hearing would occur, the matters of fact alleged, the relevant law, and the agency's legal authority to hold the hearing? Was the notice sufficient to inform the regulated entity of what it did wrong?

   a. **No**—If no, then notice was insufficient and any ensuing order would be invalid under APA § 554(b). <u>Stop here</u>.

   b. **Yes**—If yes, then notice was sufficient to fairly apprise the interested parties of the allegations. <u>Proceed to IV.B.2. below</u>.

2. Did the agency allow officials who performed investigative or prosecutorial functions supervise or oversee the ALJ who presided over the hearing?

   a. **No**—If no or if the agency head presided over the hearing, then there was no violation of the APA's separation of functions provision. <u>Proceed to IV.B.3. below</u>.

   b. **Yes**—If yes, then any ensuing order would be invalid under APA § 554(d)(2). <u>Stop here</u>.

3. Did the proponent of the order, usually the agency, have the burden of proof?

   a. **No**—If no, then any ensuing order would be invalid under APA § 556(d). <u>Stop here</u>.

   b. **Yes**—If yes, then the burden was correct. <u>Proceed to IV.B.4. below</u>.

4. Did the parties have the right to present their cases personally or through counsel, to present rebuttal evidence, and to conduct cross-examination *if necessary*?

    a.   **No**—If no and the proceeding was not one seeking benefits, one seeking an initial license, or a formal rulemaking, then any ensuing order would be invalid. <u>Stop here</u>. If the proceeding was one of the three identified, the agency may limit oral testimony and require all relevant information be submitted in writing under APA § 556(d). <u>Proceed to IV.B.5. below</u>.

    b.   **Yes**—If yes, then <u>proceed to IV.B.5. below</u>.

5.   Did any communications occur that were not on the public record and to which notice to all parties was not given, other than status reports?

    a.   **No**—If no, then no ex parte communications occurred as defined in APA § 551(14). <u>Proceed to IV.B.8. below</u>.

    b.   **Yes**—If yes, then prohibited ex parte communications may have occurred. <u>Proceed to IV.B.6. below</u> to determine whether the ex parte communications were prohibited.

6.   Did the ALJ (but not the agency or agency head) discuss a *fact in dispute* with anyone while not in the presence of all the parties in a proceeding other than one involving an application for an initial license or one challenging the validity or application of rates for public utilities and carriers? Note that the agency and agency head are allowed to make such communications under APA § 554(d)(2)(A)–(C).

    a.   **No**—If no, then <u>proceed to IV.B.7. below</u> to determine whether other communications were prohibited ex parte communications.

    b.   **Yes**—If yes, then the ALJ engaged in prohibited ex parte communications under APA § 554(d)(1). To determine the remedy, ask whether the prohibited communication was discovered while the action was pending before the agency.

        i.   **No**—If no, then the reviewing court will consider whether to void the order (or rule if formal rulemaking) by considering the following factors: (1) the gravity of the ex parte communications; (2) whether the ex parte communications may have influenced the agency's decision; (3) whether the party making the ex parte communications ultimately benefited from making them; (4) whether the contents of the ex

parte communications were known to the other side, who would thus have had an opportunity to respond; and (5) whether vacating the agency's decision would serve a useful purpose. If the order must be voided, <u>stop here</u>. If the order is not voided for this reason, <u>proceed to IV.B.7</u>.

ii. **Yes**—If yes, then the agency must cure the violation by placing the communication on the public record and must consider whether to sanction the violator under APA §§ 557(d)(1)(C)(i) & (ii). <u>Proceed to IV.B.7. below</u>. To consider whether other prohibited ex parte communications took place.

7. Did the decision maker (the ALJ, agency, or agency head) discuss *the merits of the case* with *interested persons outside the agency* while not in the presence of all the parties?

   a. **No**—If no, then no prohibited ex parte communications occurred. <u>Proceed to IV.B.8. below</u>.

   b. **Yes**—If yes, then the decision maker engaged in prohibited ex parte communications APA § 557(d)(1). To determine the remedy, ask whether the prohibited communication was discovered while the action was pending before the agency?

      i. **No**—If no, then the reviewing court will consider whether to void the order or rule by considering the following factors: (1) the gravity of the ex parte communications; (2) whether the ex parte communications may have influenced the agency's decision; (3) whether the party making the ex parte communications ultimately benefited from making them; (4) whether the contents of the ex parte communications were known to the other side, who would thus have had an opportunity to respond; and (5) whether vacating the agency's decision would serve a useful purpose. If the order must be voided, <u>stop here</u>. If the order is not voided for this reason, <u>proceed to IV.B.8. below</u>.

      ii. **Yes**—If yes, then the agency must cure the violation by placing by considering the communication on the public record and consider whether to sanction the violator under APA §§ 557(d)(1)(C)(i) & (ii). Proceed to IV.B.8. below.

8.   On appeal to the agency, in applying *de novo* review, did the agency defer to the ALJ's testimonial findings but not the derivative findings?

   a.   **No**—If no, then a reviewing court may reverse the agency's decision as not supported by substantial evidence unless the agency had a good reason for rejecting the testimonial findings. Proceed to the checklist in chapter 7 to determine whether the substance of the order is valid.

   b.   **Yes**—If yes, then a reviewing court is less likely to reverse the agency's findings as not supported by substantial evidence. Proceed to the checklist in chapter 7 to determine whether the substance of order is valid.

C. **Informal Adjudication Procedures**—Did the agency follow appropriate procedures?

   1.   Did the agency promptly decide the issue and notify the affected party?

      a.   **No**—If no, then the agency violated the APA § 552(e) and the order is invalid. Stop here.

      b.   **Yes**—If yes, the agency complied with all procedures required by the APA, but may also have to follow additional procedures to comply with the Federal Constitution or the enabling statute. Proceed to IV.C.2. below.

   2.   To determine whether Due Process applies, ask whether the regulated entity has a constitutionally protected interest.

      a.   Does the regulated entity have more than a unilateral expectation or abstract need for the interest being deprived?

         i.   **No**—If no, then the regulated entity does not have a protected property interest, but may have a protected liberty interest. Proceed to IV.C.2.b. below.

         ii. **Yes**—If yes, then the regulated entity has a protected property interest, and the agency must provide some form of a hearing. To determine what additional procedures are necessary, proceed to IV.C.3. below.

b. Will the regulated entity suffer a reputational harm and future harm as a result of the deprivation?

    i. **No**—If no, then the regulated entity does not have a protected liberty interest and, assuming the regulated entity did not have a protected property interest, has no right to any procedures other than those required by the APA. The agency's order is procedurally valid. Proceed to VII below to determine whether the substance of the order is valid.

    ii. **Yes**—If yes, then the regulated entity has a protected liberty interest, but may not have a right to a hearing. Does the regulated entity dispute the underlying facts leading to the reputational injury?

        (a). **No**—If no, then under *Codd v. Velger*[3] the regulated entity has no right to a hearing. Stop here.

        (b). **Yes**—If yes, then the agency must provide some form of a hearing. To determine what additional procedures are necessary, proceed to IV.C.3. below.

3. To determine what procedures apply when Due Process applies, ask the following questions.

    a. Do exigent circumstances prevent the agency from providing some form of a pre-deprivation hearing?

        i. **No**—If no, then the agency must provide some form of a pre-deprivation hearing. If the agency failed to do so, the order is invalid. Stop here. If the agency did so, proceed to IV.C.3.b. below to determine whether the procedures provided were constitutionally sufficient.

        ii. **Yes**—If yes, then the agency may provide a post-deprivation hearing rather than a pre-deprivation hearing. Proceed to IV.C.3.b. below to determine whether the procedures provided were constitutionally sufficient.

---

[3]   429 U.S. 627 (1977).

b.   Ask the following question for each specific procedure the regulated entity wants, such as the right to the assistance of counsel or the ability to conduct cross-examination: Does the seriousness of the harm to the individual and the risk of erroneous deprivation if the procedure is not used outweigh the administrative and fiscal burden on the agency if it is?

      i.   **No**—If no, then the agency need not provide that procedure under *Mathews v. Eldridge*,[4] and the order is procedurally valid. Proceed to VII to determine whether the substance of the order is valid.

      ii.   **Yes**—If yes, then the agency must provide the relevant procedure and any order resulting from a hearing that did not include the procedure would be invalid. Stop here.

V. DID THE AGENCY FOLLOW APPROPRIATE INFORMATION GATHERING PROCEDURES? (CHAPTER 5)

A.   **Information Gathering**—Did the agency seek information or disclose information?

    1.   **No**—If no, then return to I above. You have made a mistake in identifying the type of agency action at issue.

    2.   **Yes**—If yes, then proceed to V.B.1. below if the agency sought information and to C.1. below if the agency disclosed information.

B.   **Information Flowing to the Agency**—

    1.   Did the agency seek information in documentary or testimonial form?

      a.   **No**—If no, proceed to V.B.2. below.

      b.   **Yes**—If yes, proceed to V.B.1.c. below.

      c.   **Voluntary Nature of the Production**—Did the regulated entity voluntarily provide the information?

        i.   **No**—If no, proceed to V.B.1.d. below.

        ii.   **Yes**—If yes, then stop here. The agency can ask for information and the regulated entity can voluntarily provide that information.

---

[4]   424 U.S. 319, 335 (1976).

d. **Involuntary Production**—Did the agency go to court to compel compliance with an agency subpoena (for testimony) or subpoena *duces tecum* (for documents)?

    i. **No**—If no, <u>stop here</u>. The agency has no independent power to enforce its subpoena and must go to federal court.

    ii. **Yes**—If yes, then <u>proceed to V.B.1.e. below</u>.

e. **Motion to Quash Subpoena**—

    i. Did the agency prove that it has statutory authority to issue the subpoena?

        (a). No—If no, <u>stop here</u>. The court should quash the subpoena because the agency does not have statutory authority to issue the subpoena.

        (b). Yes—If yes, <u>proceed to V.B.1.e.ii. below</u>.

    ii. Did the agency prove that (1) the subpoena was issued for a congressionally authorized purpose, (2) the information sought was relevant to an authorized purpose, and (3) the information sought was adequately described?

        (a). No—If no, <u>stop here</u>. The court should quash the subpoena because it violates the Fourth Amendment of the Constitution.

        (b). Yes—If yes, <u>proceed to V.B.1.e.iii. below</u>.

    iii. Did the person moving to quash the subpoena prove that it would compel an individual, not a business, to testify *orally* against himself and that testifying would lead to criminal prosecution?

        (a). No—If no, proceed to V.B.1.e.iv. below.

        (b). Yes—If yes, stop here. The court should quash the subpoena because it violates the Fifth Amendment of the Constitution.

    iv. Did the person moving to quash the subpoena prove that it would compel an individual, not a business, to produce voluntarily created documents, not involuntarily created documents, and that the very act of production could serve as proof that a crime occurred?

      (a). No—If no, then the court should not quash the subpoena, and the regulated entity must comply. <u>Stop here.</u>

      (b). Yes—If yes, <u>stop here</u>. The court should quash the subpoena because it violates the Fifth Amendment of the Constitution. But this is likely the wrong answer because the act of production doctrine is so narrow you have likely missed one of the elements.

2.   Did the agency seek to inspect a regulated entity?

    a.   **No**—If no, you have made a mistake. <u>Return to V.A.1.</u>

    b.   **Yes**—If yes, <u>proceed to V.B.2.c. below.</u>

    c.   **Voluntary Nature of the Production**—Did the regulated entity voluntarily allow the inspection?

      i.   **No**—If no, <u>proceed to V.B.2.d. below.</u>

      ii.   **Yes**—If yes, then <u>Stop Here</u>. The agency can ask for to inspect and the regulated entity can voluntarily allow the inspection.

    d.   **Involuntary Production**—Does the agency need a warrant to conduct the inspection?

      i.   Is the location to be searched in plain view?

        (a). No—If no, <u>proceed to V.B.2.d.ii. below.</u>

        (b). Yes—If yes, then <u>stop here</u>. A warrant is not needed under the Fourth Amendment. The search is valid.

      ii.   Is there an emergency that justifies a search?

        (a). No—If no, <u>proceed to V.B.2.d.iii. below.</u>

        (b). Yes—If yes, then <u>stop here</u>. A warrant is not needed under the Fourth Amendment. The search is valid.

      iii.   Is the search conducted pursuant to informed consent?

        (a). No—If no, <u>proceed to V.B.2.d.iv. below.</u>

        (b). Yes—If yes, then <u>stop here</u>. A warrant is not needed under the Fourth Amendment. The search is valid.

iv. Is the search of a closely regulated business, such as a liquor dealer, weapon dealer, stone quarries, or dismantling junkyard?

    (a). No—If no, then <u>stop here</u>. A warrant is required. However, the agency need only show administrative probable cause, meaning the statute or regulation allows periodic inspections and this inspection falls within the statutory parameters.

    (b). Yes—If yes, then <u>stop here</u>. A warrant is not needed under the Fourth Amendment. The search is valid.

C. Information Flowing from the Agency—

  1. Did a requester seek information from the agency?

    a.   No—If no, <u>proceed to V.C.2. below</u>. FOIA does not apply.

    b.   Yes—If yes, <u>proceed to V.C.1.c. below</u>.

    c.   Does one of the nine exceptions in APA § 552(b)(1)–(9) apply?

      i.   **No**—If no, <u>stop here</u>. FOIA applies, and the information must be disclosed. The requester can sue in federal court; if the requester substantially prevails, the court may award costs and attorneys' fees.

      ii.   **Yes**—If yes, <u>stop here</u>. The agency is allowed to withhold the information.

  2. Did the agency hold a meeting with a quorum of its members, to deliberate, which resulted in the disposition of official agency business that was not open to the public?

    a.   No—If no, <u>proceed to V.C.3. below</u>. The Sunshine Act does not apply, and the meeting did not need to be open to the public.

    b.   Yes—If yes, <u>proceed to V.C.2.c. below</u>.

    c.   Does one of the ten exceptions in APA § 552b(c)(1)–(10) apply?

      i.   **No**—If no, <u>stop here</u>. The Sunshine Act applies, and the meeting should have been open to the public. If the meeting has not yet occurred, anyone can use to have the meeting opened. If the meeting already occurred, the only judicial remedy is likely to be a transcript of the illegally closed meeting, costs, and attorneys' fees.

      ii.   **Yes**—If yes, <u>stop here</u>. The agency is allowed to conduct a closed meeting.

3. Did the agency hold a meeting with "any committee, board, commission, council, conference, panel, task force, or other similar group, or any subcommittee ... established by statute or reorganization plan, ... established or utilized by the President, or ... established or utilized by one or more agencies" that was not open to the public?

    a.   **No**—If no, <u>stop here</u>. FACA does not apply, and the meeting did not need to be open to the public.

    b.   **Yes**—If yes, <u>proceed to V.C.3.c. below</u>.

    c.   Does one of the exceptions in FACA §§ 10(b) & (d) apply?

        i.   **No**—If no, <u>stop here</u>. FACA applies, and the meeting should have been open to the public. However, FACA does not provide for judicial review.

    b.   **Yes**—If yes, <u>stop here</u>. The agency is allowed to conduct a closed meeting.

VI. IS JUDICIAL REVIEW OF THE AGENCY'S ACTION AVAILABLE? (CHAPTER 6)

A. Jurisdiction—

  1.   Does the enabling statute give federal courts jurisdiction?

    a.   **No**—If no, then jurisdiction must be found based on the federal question statute, 28 U.S.C. § 1331. The APA does not provide jurisdiction. <u>Proceed to VI.A.1.2. below</u>.

    b.   **Yes**—If yes, then the court has jurisdiction. <u>Proceed to VI.B. below</u> to see if the plaintiff has a cause of action.

  2.   Does the plaintiff allege a claim that "aris[es] under the Constitution, law, or treaties of the United States"?

    a.   **No**—If no, then the court does not have jurisdiction. <u>Stop here</u>. But this answer is likely wrong because most challenges to agency action will involve questions about federal law.

    b. **Yes**—If yes, then the court has jurisdiction. <u>Proceed to VI.B. below</u> to see if the plaintiff has a cause of action.

B. **Cause of Action—**

    1. Does the enabling statute provide that anyone adversely affected by the agency's action may file an action challenging its validity or otherwise provide a cause of action?

        a. **No**—If no, then the enabling statute does not provide a cause of action, but the APA may. <u>Proceed to VI.B.2. below</u>.

        b. **Yes**—If yes, then the plaintiff has a cause of action. <u>Proceed to VI.C. below</u> to see if the plaintiff has standing.

    2. Does APA § 702 provide the plaintiff with a cause of action?

        a. **Agency Action**—Did the agency either act in a discrete manner or fail to act when required to act?

            i. **No**—If no, then there is no agency action. <u>Stop here</u>.

            ii. **Yes**—If yes, then there was agency action. <u>Proceed to VI.B.2.b.</u> to determine whether the statute precludes review implicitly or explicitly.

        b. **Statutory Preclusion—**

            i. Does the statute explicitly preclude the court from reviewing plaintiff(s)'s claim?

                (a). **No**—If no, then Congress did not explicitly precluded review but may have implicitly precluded review. <u>Proceed to VI.B.2.b.ii</u>.

                (b). **Yes**—If yes, then the court cannot hear the case. <u>Stop here</u>. But this answer is likely wrong because Congress rarely precludes review explicitly.

            ii. Is it fairly discernible in the statutory scheme (meaning the statute's language, structure, purpose, and legislative history) that Congress implicitly precluded the federal courts from reviewing plaintiff's claim?

(a). No—If no, then Congress did not implicitly preclude review. <u>Proceed to VI.B.2.c.</u> to determine whether the issue is committed to agency discretion.

(b). Yes—If yes, then ask (1) would a finding of preclusion foreclose all meaningful judicial review, (2) is the federal suit wholly collateral to a statute's review provisions, and (3) are the claims outside of the agency's expertise?

— **Yes**—If you answered yes to any of these questions, then Congress did not implicitly preclude review. <u>Proceed to VI.B.2.c.</u> to determine whether the issue is committed to agency discretion

— **No**—If you answered no to all of the questions, then Congress precluded review, and the court cannot hear the case. <u>Stop here</u>.

c. **Committed to Agency Discretion**—Does the statute provide meaningful standards with which to measure the agency's action?

i. **No**—If no, then Congress committed this particular decision to the agency, and the court cannot hear the case (assuming that is the only challenge). <u>Stop here</u>. But this answer is likely wrong because judicial review is preferred.

ii. **Yes**—If yes, then the plaintiff has a cause of action that the court can hear. <u>Proceed to VI.C. below</u> to determine whether the plaintiff(s) has standing.

C. Standing—

1. **Prudential Standing**—Is the plaintiff an association suing on behalf of the public rather than for its own personal injury?

a. **No**—If no, then plaintiff must be suing directly (whether it is the association suing for its own harm or a plaintiff suing for his/her/its own harm). Associational standing is irrelevant. <u>Proceed to</u>

VI.C.2. below to determine whether the plaintiff has constitutional standing.

b. **Yes**—If yes, then the plaintiff must meet the associational standing requirements. Proceed to VI.C.1.c. below.

c. **Associational Standing**—

    i. Assuming an association is suing, does the lawsuit relate to the purposes of the association?

        (a). No—If no, then the association has no standing pursuant to prudential standing. Stop here. But this answer is likely wrong because associations generally only sue for issues related to their mission.

        (b). Yes—If yes, then the association meets one element of associational standing. Proceed to VI.C.1.c.ii. below to see if the association meets the other elements.

    ii. Assuming an association is suing, can the lawsuit proceed without an individual's participation, meaning that the lawsuit is for injunctive or declaratory relief only?

        (a). No—If no, then the association has no standing pursuant to prudential standing. Stop here. But this answer is likely wrong because associations generally only sue for declaratory and injunctive relief.

        (b). Yes—If yes, then the association meets another element of associational standing. Proceed to VI.C.1.c.iii. below to see if the association meets the remaining element.

    iii. Assuming an association is suing, does one member have constitutional standing, meaning injury in fact, causation, and redressability? (you will need to work through VI.C.2. below, then return here).

        (a). No—If no, then the association has no standing pursuant to prudential standing. Stop here.

        (b). Yes—If yes, then the association meets the prudential standing requirements. Proceed

to VI.C.3. below to see if the plaintiff meets
the statutory standing requirements.

2. **Constitutional Standing—**

   a. **Injury in Fact—**

      i. Does the plaintiff allege that he or she would be
          directly injured economically (*e.g.*, by a fine) or
          physically by the agency?

          (a). No—If no, then plaintiff must be alleging an
          indirect injury. Proceed to C.2.a.ii. below.

          (b). Yes—If yes, the plaintiff has an injury in
          fact that is concrete and particularized,
          which is one element of constitutional
          standing. Proceed to C.2.b. below to
          determine whether plaintiff can show
          causation.

      ii. Does the plaintiff allege only that he or she
          suffered a procedural injury, meaning the agency
          failed to follow a legally required procedure?

          (a). No—If no, then plaintiff must be alleging a
          different indirect injury. Proceed to C.2.a.iii.
          below.

          (b). Yes—If yes, the plaintiff does not have
          injury in fact, which is one element of
          constitutional standing. Stop here.

      iii. Does the plaintiff allege that he or she suffered
           an informational injury, meaning the agency
           failed to disclose information it was required to
           disclose to this plaintiff?

           (a). No—If no, then plaintiff must be alleging a
           different indirect injury. Proceed to C.2.a.iv.
           below.

           (b). Yes—If yes, then plaintiff has injury in fact.
           Proceed to C.2.b. below to determine
           whether plaintiff can show causation.

      iv. Does the plaintiff allege that he or she suffered a
          recreational, aesthetic, or environmental injury?

          (a). No—If no, then the plaintiff does not have
          injury in fact, which is one element of
          constitutional standing. Stop here. This

answer is likely wrong; plaintiff must be alleging one of the injuries above.

(b). Yes—If yes, then ask whether the plaintiff can show concrete plans to visit the location or see the nature to be harmed in the near future?

— **No**—If no, then the plaintiff does not have injury in fact, which is one element of constitutional standing. <u>Stop here</u>.

— **Yes**—If yes, then plaintiff has injury in fact. <u>Proceed to C.2.b. below</u> to see if the plaintiff can show causation.

b. **Causation**—Can the plaintiff show that the alleged illegal action by the agency caused the plaintiff's harm?

i. **No**—If no, then the harm was likely caused by a third party, and plaintiff cannot show causation, which is one element of constitutional standing. <u>Stop here</u>.

ii. **Yes**—If yes, then the plaintiff can show causation. <u>Proceed to C.2.c. below</u> to determine whether plaintiff can show redressability.

c. **Redressability**—Can the plaintiff show that a favorable decision will remedy the plaintiff's harm?

i. **No**—If no, then the harm cannot be remedied by the agency, and the plaintiff cannot show redressability, which is one element of constitutional standing. <u>Stop here</u>.

ii. **Yes**—If yes, the plaintiff can show redressability, which is one element of constitutional standing. <u>Proceed to C.3. below</u> to determine whether plaintiff meets statutory standing requirements.

3. **Statutory Standing (Zone of Interests)**—Is plaintiff bringing suit pursuant to APA § 702?

a. **No**—If no, then the plaintiff must be bringing suit pursuant to the enabling statute, the zone of interest requirement does not apply because the plaintiff must be within the protection of the relevant statute. <u>Proceed to VI.D. below</u> to determine whether plaintiff's lawsuit meets the timing requirements.

b. **Yes**—If yes, then the plaintiff must demonstrate that he/she/it is "arguably" within the zone of interests the specific statute was meant to protect. Can plaintiff meet this burden?

    i. **No**—If no, then the plaintiff cannot meet statutory standing requirements. <u>Stop here</u>.

    ii. **Yes**—If yes, the plaintiff can meet the statutory standing requirements. <u>Proceed to VI.D. below</u> to determine whether plaintiff's lawsuit meets the timing requirements.

D. Timing—

1. Is the plaintiff suing pursuant to APA § 704?

    a. **No**—If no, then the common law doctrine of finality, exhaustion, and ripeness may apply. <u>Stop here</u> and apply those doctrines. But in an Administrative Law course, it is more likely that you will be tested on these doctrines as codified in APA § 704.

    b. **Yes**—If yes, then <u>proceed to VI.D.2. below</u> to determine whether now is the appropriate time for a court to hear the plaintiff's claim.

2. **Finality**—

    a. Is the action the culmination of the agency's decisionmaking process?

        i. **No**—if no, then the agency's action is not final, and the court cannot hear the case at this time. <u>Stop here</u>.

        ii. **Yes**—If yes, then the agency's action meets one of the finality elements. <u>Proceed to VI.D.2.b. below</u> to see if it meets the other.

    b. Is the agency action one from which "rights or obligations have been determined,' or from which 'legal consequences will flow?' "

        i. **No**—if no, then the agency's action is not final, and the court cannot hear the case at this time. <u>Stop here</u>.

        ii. **Yes**—If yes, then the agency's action is final. <u>Proceed to VI.D.3. below</u> to see if the plaintiff meets the exhaustion requirements.

3. **Exhaustion**—Is the plaintiff required to exhaust administrative remedies before suing in federal court and failed to do so?

    a. Does the enabling statute expressly require the plaintiff to exhaust administrative remedies?

        i. **No**—If no, then the statute does not require the plaintiff to exhaust administrative remedies. <u>Proceed to VI.D.3.b. below</u> to determine whether a regulation requires the plaintiff to exhaust administrative remedies.

        ii. **Yes**—If yes, then the plaintiff must exhaust administrative remedies prior to filing suit. You may wish to note here that the common law exceptions to exhaustion likely to do not apply because Congress did not codify them within APA § 704. <u>Stop here</u>.

    b. Does the agency's own regulation expressly require the plaintiff to exhaust administrative remedies and stay its action pending administrative appeal?

        i. **No**—If no, then the regulation does not require the plaintiff to exhaust administrative remedies. <u>Proceed to VI.D.4. below</u> to determine whether the action is ripe.

        ii. **Yes**—If yes, then the plaintiff must exhaust administrative remedies prior to filing suit. You may wish to note here that the common law exceptions to exhaustion likely to do not apply because Congress did not codify them within APA § 704. <u>Stop here</u>.

4. **Ripeness**—Is the case sufficiently developed for judicial review?

    a. Does the case involve purely legal issues?

        i. **No**—If no, then the case is not ripe, and the court should not hear it at this time. <u>Stop here</u>.

        ii. **Yes**—If yes, then the case meets one of the ripeness elements. <u>Proceed to VI.D.4.b. below</u> to determine whether case meets both elements.

    b. Will the plaintiff actually be harmed if judicial review is delayed?

i.   **No**—If no, then the case is not ripe, and the court should not hear it at this time. Stop here.

ii. **Yes**—If yes, then the case if ripe for judicial review at this time. Proceed to VII to determine the appropriate standard of review the court will apply.

VII.   WHAT STANDARD OF REVIEW APPLIES? (CHAPTER 7)

A.   **Type of Finding/Question:**

1.   Is the court reviewing a finding of fact or policy?

a.   No—If no, then proceed to VII.A.2. below.

b.   Yes—If yes, then ask whether the agency made its finding as a part of a formal adjudication or a formal rulemaking.

i.   Yes—If yes, then the reviewing court will review the agency's finding using the substantial evidence standard. Proceed to VII.B.1. below.

ii. No—If no, then the reviewing court will review the agency's finding using the arbitrary and capricious standard. Proceed to VII.B.2. below.

2.   Is the court reviewing a finding of law?

a.   No—If no, then proceed to VII.A.3. below.

b.   Yes—If yes, then ask the following:

i.   Is the agency interpreting language in a constitution or contract?

(a). Yes—If yes, then the reviewing court will review the agency's interpretation *de novo*. Stop here.

(b). No—If no, then proceed to VII.A.2.b.ii.

ii. Is the agency interpreting language in its own regulation?

(a). Yes—If yes, then *Auer* deference may apply. Proceed to VII.B.5. below.

(b). No—If no, then proceed to VII.A.2.b.iii.

iii. Is the agency interpreting language in a statute that the agency administers?

       (a). Yes—If yes, then ask whether the agency made its finding as a part of a formal adjudication, a formal rulemaking, or a notice-and-comment rulemaking.

         — **Yes**—If yes, then the reviewing court will review the agency's finding using *Chevron* analysis. <u>Proceed to VII.B.4. below</u>.

         — **No**—If no, then the reviewing court will review the agency's finding using *Skidmore* analysis. <u>Proceed to VII.B.3. below</u>.

       (b). No—If no, then the reviewing court will review the agency's interpretation of a statute it does not administer *de novo*. <u>Stop here</u>.

  3. Is the court reviewing a mixed finding of law/law application?

      a. **No**—If no, then <u>return to VII.A.1</u>. You have made an error.

      b. **Yes**—If yes, then follow the analysis for findings of fact (VII.A.1.) for that portion of the finding and follow the analysis for findings of law (VII.A.2.) for that portion of the finding.

B. **Standards of Review:** (After identifying the standard of review, apply it).

  1. If the substantial evidence standard of review applies, then ask whether the evidence in the record would allow a reasonable person to make the same finding that the agency made.

      a. **No**—If no, then the court will reject the agency's finding. <u>Stop here</u>.

      b. **Yes**—If yes, then the court will uphold the agency's finding. <u>Stop here</u>. Substantial evidence is defined as such relevant evidence as a reasonable mind might accept as adequate to support a conclusion.

  2. If the arbitrary and capricious standard of review applies, ask the following: was the agency's decision (1) based on a consideration of all the relevant factors, and (2) free of clear error? (Both elements must be satisfied).

a. **No**—If no, then the court will reject the agency's finding. <u>Stop here</u>.

b. **Yes**—If yes, then the court will uphold the agency's finding. <u>Stop here</u>. A non-arbitrary and capricious decision is one that was based on a consideration of all the relevant factors and has no clear errors of judgment.

3. If *Skidmore* analysis applies, then balance the following three factors: (1) the thoroughness evident in the agency's consideration of the issue, (2) the validity of the agency's reasoning for its interpretation, and (3) the consistency of the agency's interpretation over time. Does the balancing of these factors support the agency's finding?

   a. **No**—If no, then the court will reject the agency's interpretation. <u>Stop here</u>.

   b. **Yes**—If yes, then the court will uphold the agency's interpretation because the agency was persuasive. <u>Stop here</u>.

4. If *Chevron* analysis applies, then ask the following questions:

   a. Has a court already interpreted the same language differently from the agency?

      i. **No**—If no, <u>Proceed to VII.4.b. below</u>. Because there is no prior court interpretation, the agency is not bound by one.

      ii. **Yes**—If yes, then ask whether the prior court reached its interpretation at *Chevron*'s first step?

         (a). No—If no, then the prior court reached its interpretation based on its conclusion of what was the best interpretation and not based on what Congress demanded. The agency is free to reach a different interpretation so long as that interpretation is reasonable under *Chevron*'s second step. <u>Proceed to VII.4.c</u>.

         (b). Yes—If yes, the prior judicial interpretation controls because Congress has spoken, and the court will reject any agency interpretation that is not consistent with the prior judicial interpretation. <u>Stop here</u>.

b. Using the traditional tools of statutory interpretation, apply *Chevron*'s first step by asking whether Congress has spoken directly to the precise issue before the court (congressional intent)?

    i. **No**—If no, <u>Proceed to VII.4.c.</u> If Congress does not have a specific intent as to the language at issue, the Congress impliedly delegated resolution of the statute's meaning to the agency.

    ii. **Yes**—If yes, ask whether the agency's interpretation is consistent with congressional intent.

        (a). **No**—If no, then the agency's interpretation is invalid because it conflicts with Congressional intent. <u>Stop here</u>. (You may wish to argue in the alternative and reach *Chevron*'s second step).

        (b). **Yes**—If yes, then the agency's interpretation is valid because it is consistent with congressional intent. <u>Stop here</u>. (You may wish to argue in the alternative and reach *Chevron*'s second step).

c. If Congress has not directly spoken to the precise issue before the court, apply *Chevron*'s second step by asking whether the agency has offered a reasoned explanation for why it chose that interpretation and whether the interpretation is reasonable?

    i. **No**—If no, then the agency's interpretation is invalid because is unreasonable or the process was arbitrary and capricious. <u>Stop here</u>.

    ii. **Yes**—If yes, then the agency's interpretation is valid. <u>Stop here</u>.

5. If *Auer* analysis applies, then ask the following questions:

a. Did the agency simply parrot the statutory language in its first regulation and then interpret the parroting language in its second regulation?

    i. **No**—If no, <u>proceed to VII.B.5.b.</u>

    ii. **Yes**—If yes, the agency's interpretation is not entitled to *Auer* analysis. If the agency's second regulation is legislative, then *Chevron* analysis applies. <u>Return to VII.B.4. above.</u> If the agency's second regulation is non-legislative, then

Skidmore analysis applies. <u>Return to VII.B.3. above</u>.

b. Is the agency's interpretation plainly erroneous or inconsistent with the regulation it is interpreting?

   i. **No**—If no, then the agency's interpretation of its own regulation is valid. <u>Stop here</u>.

   ii. **Yes**—If yes, then the agency's interpretation of its own regulation is invalid. <u>Stop here</u>.

ILLUSTRATIVE PROBLEMS

■ LONG ESSAY PROBLEM 8.1 ■

Climate change has been in the news lately, as more and more scientific studies suggest that humans are causing the changes in climate seen in recent decades. Shrinking polar ice caps, changes in global weather patterns, increases in atmospheric carbon dioxide, and rising average temperatures worldwide suggest there is a very real problem. The scientific evidence is by no means conclusive, but there is a growing public consensus in the United States that climate change is an issue the federal government should no longer ignore.

After a particularly hot summer and autumn, in January 20XX, Congress enacted legislation addressing climate change: Congress overwhelmingly passed the "Handling Environmental Adjustments in Temperature Act of 20XX" ("the HEAT Act") in October. Sensing the public mood, and reassured by the bill's sponsor during the floor debates that the bill was not intended to target any specific industry, the President signed the bill on October 28, 20XX. The law became effective on December 31, 20XX.

The HEAT Act provides, in relevant part, as follows:

Section 1: Findings. The Congress makes the following findings:

(a) Scientific studies have documented that average temperatures are increasing globally due to carbon dioxide and other noxious emissions;

(b) This phenomenon, popularly known as "climate change" and "global warming" is a significant danger to world environmental stability and is the cause of severe hurricanes, tornadoes, floods, and other catastrophic events;

(c)   The United States, as leader of the free world, has a moral and ethical duty to combat the adverse effects of climate change;

(d)   At the same time, continued growth of the U.S. economy is of paramount importance so no one industry should bear the burden of remedying this danger.

Section 2: In light of these findings, the U.S. Environmental Protection Agency ("EPA") shall have the power, after opportunity for a full public hearing in which all interested parties may participate, to issue rules and regulations to reduce emissions of any industry that contributes to climate change to protect the general welfare of the Nation consistently with the findings in Section 1.

Section 3: The EPA may also seek enforcement individually against any person who does not comply with regulations promulgated by the EPA pursuant to the HEAT Act. Such enforcement actions shall be undertaken only after opportunity for an agency hearing on the record in which interested parties may participate.

Section 4: Any violation of this Act shall be punishable by a fine not exceeding US $50,000, imprisonment not exceeding 3 years, or both.

The HEAT Act does not define "any industry that contributes to climate change" in Section 2. Nor does the lengthy legislative history contain any discussion of which industries Congress intended to be covered. As noted above, the bill's sponsor said during the House floor debates, "No one industry will bear this burden alone." However, the legislative history makes repeated mention of Congress's concern with carbon dioxide emissions and methane gasses and with the effect of those pollutants on climate change.

In April of the year after the HEAT Act was signed into law, the EPA drafted new regulations to implement the HEAT Act's provisions. As part of this process, the EPA reviewed existing scientific evidence on climate change. The EPA's research revealed that while there was general scientific agreement that climate change was occurring, there was no scientific consensus as to the *cause*. That is, while many relevant scientific studies suggested that climate change was at least partly caused by human industrial activity, a smaller number of studies concluded that climate change was a cyclical climate change pattern that had nothing to do with human factors.

Furthermore, even those scientific studies that concluded that human factors were contributing to climate change did not fully agree on exactly which human factors were involved. In other words, while most of the scientific studies suggested that *carbon dioxide* emissions by industries were the most significant human-caused factor in climate change, there were a few isolated studies that suggested that *methane* gas emissions by agricultural activities were another significant human-caused factor in climate change.

In the U.S., meat production increasingly relies on concentrated forms of agriculture such as cattle feedlots, hog feedlots, and poultry farms (for chickens and turkeys). These forms of agri-business are admirably efficient in producing low-cost meat for consumers, but they produce enormous amounts of animal waste. Animal waste, of course, produces large amounts of methane as it decomposes. And the decomposition of large amounts of methane causes a lot of heat, impacting climate change.

The EPA issued a detailed Notice of Proposed Rulemaking ("NPRM") on May 1. The NPRM, which was over 200 pages long, contained the following relevant language:

> **The EPA finds** that available scientific evidence irrefutably points to climate change as being caused largely by human activity. Carbon dioxide and methane scrubbers are the most efficient at lowering carbon dioxide and methane gas emissions. The evidence is also clear that such emissions must be no more than 50 parts per billion for climate change to be reduced. Accordingly, the EPA proposes to promulgate the following "Geo-Atmospheric Standards" ("GAS") Regulation:
>
> > **GAS section 1:** All companies whose manufacturing or production activities produce carbon dioxide or methane gas shall install carbon dioxide and methane scrubbers at their own expense as part of their air ventilation systems, to capture carbon dioxide and methane gasses within their facilities and reduce emissions of these gasses from these facilities to no more than 50 parts per billion.
>
> The EPA will accept comments on these regulations from interested parties until July 1. Comments should be submitted to . . . [the NPRM lists the name and address where comments should be submitted].

The potential breadth of this proposed rule resulted in a flurry of comments to the EPA. Various industries—notably those involved in carbon dioxide emissions such as car manufacturers—

vociferously objected to the proposed regulations. There were a few comments from the poultry and pork industries objecting to the strict requirements. These industries were concerned that the cost of implementing the regulation would put them out of business compared to the small impact on the environment. In contrast, no beef producers submitted comments to the EPA about the proposed regulation. In the words of one beef producer, "the scientific data on methane gas and climate change is pretty weak, and we're not wasting our time or money on submitting comments to the EPA even though the proposed regulation might impact our industry."

On September 1, the EPA issued a comprehensive Notice of Final Rulemaking and "Statement of Basis and Purpose" (collectively, the "SOBP") explaining the final GAS Regulation. The SOPB is 300 pages long and contains a detailed statement regarding the background of the proposed rule, summaries of the public comments received on the NPRM, and the EPA's responses to these comments. The SOBP contains the following relevant language regarding the GAS Regulations being adopted by the EPA:

> **The EPA finds** that available scientific evidence irrefutably suggests that the primary contributor to climate change is methane gas emissions by cattle, especially in large feedlots. Methane scrubbers are an efficient method to lower methane gas emissions; additionally, keeping cattle indoors will also lower emissions. The evidence is also clear that such emissions must be no more than 50 parts per billion for climate change to be reduced. Accordingly, the EPA issues the following "Geo-Atmospheric Standards" ("GAS") Regulation:
>
>> **GAS section 1:** All U.S. cattle feedlots shall keep their cattle in indoor facilities that have been rendered appropriately airtight to prevent the escape of methane gasses into the atmosphere.
>>
>> **GAS section 2:** All U.S. cattle feedlots shall install methane scrubbers as part of their air ventilation systems to capture methane gasses within their facilities and reduce methane emissions to no more than 50 parts per billion.
>>
>> **GAS section 3:** To allow cattle feedlots to come into compliance with this regulation, it shall take effect beginning in September 20XX. No enforcement actions shall commence before that date. After that

date, any cattle feedlot found to be in violation of this regulation will be fined $10,000 per day of violation.

The EPA offered no data to support any of its findings. There are no other relevant regulations.

Needless to say, beef producers, who own cattle feedlots, are upset about this regulation. You are a junior associate in the law firm of Huey, Duey, & Luey. Your firm has been hired as counsel for the Beef Producers of America ("BPA"), which wants to challenge the validity of the GAS Regulation. How would you answer the following questions?

QUESTION 1

Steve Duey and David Luey are two senior partners in your firm. One Friday at 4:45 p.m. they walk into your office. Duey says, "I hear you took Administrative Law in law school. That's good, because we didn't. So we need a memo about the BPA matter on our desks by Monday at 9:00 a.m. Have a great weekend!"

The specific questions Duey and Luey want you to address in the memorandum are as follows:

(a) Does the HEAT Act unconstitutionally delegate authority to the EPA? Why or why not?

(b) If BPA wished to bring suit challenging the constitutionality of the delegation to the EPA before the rule takes effect, would the case survive a *reviewability* challenge? Please explain. Assume the BPA is seeking only injunctive and declaratory relief.

QUESTION 2

You work all weekend on the memo and get it to Duey and Luey Monday morning. The memo then sits on their desks all week until the following Friday at 4:52 p.m., when David Luey walks into your office and says, "Great work on the first BPA memo. But now Duey and I have some more questions. We've got golf plans for the weekend, so you'll need to take care of this for us."

This time, the partners have the following questions about how BPA might challenge the EPA's GAS Regulations. Your answers are of course due by 9:00 a.m. Monday.

(a) Should the EPA have proceeded by formal rather than informal rulemaking? Please explain, being sure to identify the appropriate standard of review.

(b) Assuming the action is subject to judicial review, would the EPA's decision to limit the GAS Regulation to Beef producers survive a *procedural* challenge? Please explain.

QUESTION 3

You worked all weekend (again) and finished the second memo after an all-nighter on Sunday. The next Friday, senior partner Lisa Huey walks into your office at 4:59 p.m. and says, "Great work on the BPA matter. Got one more question for you. I need an answer by Monday at 9:00 a.m. sharp. I'm going to Hilton Head for the weekend." Huey's questions are as follows:

    (a)   Assuming this action is subject to judicial review, would the EPA's *factual* findings in its final rule survive a legal challenge? Please explain, being sure to identify the appropriate standard of review.

    (b)   Assuming this action is subject to judicial review, would the EPA's *interpretation* that "any industry that contributes to climate change" provides the agency with the power to regulate only one industry, specifically, cattle feedlots, survive a legal challenge? Please explain, being sure to identify the appropriate standard of review.

Analysis[5]

Before answering the individual questions, 1–3, you should begin by asking yourself whether the question involved an agency and agency action (Checklist I.A. & I.B.) and, if so, what kind of agency action was involved (Checklist I.C.). These questions are foundational and must precede every question you analyze, even if you do not include your analysis in your answer (although you may win some brownie points by doing so).

Here, the EPA is an authority of the United States government and it issued a regulation; thus, an agency and agency action were involved. Because the EPA promulgated a regulation, is the APA's rulemaking procedures apply. So, turn to Chapter 2's checklist for Question 1.

ANALYSIS FOR QUESTION 1

1(a): The issue in Question 1(a) is whether the statute unconstitutionally delegates legislative power to the agency. Turning to II.C.1. in the checklist above, you need to analyze

---

[5]   Be aware that the answers below are necessarily succinct and do not cite relevant case law or the APA. The purpose is to show you how to use the checklist not how to draft a perfect answer. Hence, be sure to expand these arguments much more fully and cite relevant law.

whether Congress provided an *intelligible principle* to guide the EPA's decisionmaking. Examples of intelligible principles include "requisite to protect the public health," "necessary to avoid an imminent hazard to the public safety," "adequately assures . . . that no employee will suffer any impairment of health," and "[not] unduly or unnecessarily complicate[d]."

In analyzing this question, be sure that you correctly identify the section of the statute that applies. Here, the action is rulemaking, so Section 2 of the HEAT Act is the relevant section. Section 2 of the HEAT Act authorizes the EPA to issue rules to reduce emissions of industries that contribute to climate change "to protect the general welfare of the nation." This intelligible principle is sufficiently similar to those intelligible principles that have survived Supreme Court scrutiny in this area in the past. Hence, the HEAT Act likely is constitutional.

1(b):   The issue in Question 1(b) is whether the BPA would be able to seek judicial review at this time (pre-enforcement review). Turning to VI.A.1. in the checklist above, you should ask first whether a federal court would have jurisdiction over this particular claim. In this case, the relevant statute does not appear to grant the federal court jurisdiction, the APA does not grant jurisdiction; hence, jurisdiction must be found based on the federal question statute, 28 U.S.C. § 1331. The BPA is alleging a claim that arises under a statute of the United States, the HEAT Act; thus, the court would have jurisdiction.

Second, you should determine whether the enabling statute gives the BPA the right to sue ("a cause of action") (VI.B.). Here, the enabling statute does not provide that anyone adversely affected by the agency's action may file an action challenging its validity or otherwise provide a cause of action (VI.B.1.a.); hence, you should turn to the APA to see if it provides the BPA with a cause of action (VI.B.2.). To determine whether APA § 702 provides the BPA with a cause of action, you should conclude that the EPA acted in a discrete manner—it issued a regulation (agency action: VI.B.2.a.); there are no facts suggesting that the HEAT Act either explicitly or implicitly precludes judicial review (implied/express preclusion: VI.B.2.b.); and there are no facts suggesting that the HEAT Act does not provide meaningful standards with which to measure the EPA's action, meaning Congress did not commit this this particular decision to the agency (VI.B.2.c.).

Third, you must determine whether the BPA has standing to bring this claim: constitutional, prudential, and statutory standing (VI.C.). As for prudential standing, the BPA is an association suing on behalf of its members; thus, the BPA must meet the three associational standing requirements (VI.C.1.c.). Here, the lawsuit relates to the purposes of the organization: the organization represents beef producers generally and this regulation affects beef producers (VI.C.1.c.i). Moreover, the lawsuit seeks declaratory and injunctive relief only, so an individual member's participation is not required. (VI.C.1.c.ii.). The final associational standing question is whether one of the BPA's members has constitutional standing: meaning injury in fact, causation, and redressability. (VI.C.1.c.iii.)

Here, one of BPA's members, a beef producer, can demonstrate that it would likely be fined if the regulation takes effect. Such an injury would be sufficiently concrete and particularized and imminent. So, injury in fact is met. (VI.C.2.a.i.). Second, BPA could show that the alleged illegal action by the agency, the regulation, will cause the member's harm (VI.C.2.b.), and that the harm will be redressed if the regulation is not issued (VI.C.2.c.). Thus, causation and redressability are met.

Next comes statutory standing (VI.C.3.). The BPA is likely to be able to demonstrate that its members are "arguably" within the zone of interests of the HEAT Act as an industry that contributes to climate change. Hence, statutory standing is likely met.

Fourth, you must determine whether the BPA can bring this particular claim at this time. The BPA would be suing pursuant to the APA, so section 704's finality and exhaustion doctrines apply (VI.D.1.b.). Additionally, the common law doctrine of ripeness applies. Regarding finality (VI.D.2.), a final regulation is the culmination of the agency's decisionmaking process and regulation is one from which rights legal consequences will flow (VI.D.2.a. & b.); the industry will have to comply or risk $10,000 per day fines. Hence, finality is met.

Regarding exhaustion (VI.D.3.), the HEAT Act does not require the BPA to exhaust administrative remedies, and there is no relevant administrative regulation (VI.D.3.i.). Hence, exhaustion is not required in this case.

Regarding ripeness (VI.D.4.), you must analyze (1) whether the claims are purely legal and (2) whether the beef producers will be harmed if judicial review is delayed. Turning to analyze the first ripeness factor, you should conclude that the BPA's challenge relates only to the constitutionality of the delegation. This question is purely legal and no further factual development would be necessary (VI.D.4.a.i.).

Turning to analyze the second ripeness factor, you should conclude that the beef producers may well be harmed if judicial review is delayed. Every day that they fail to comply with the regulation, they are subject to $10,000 fine. Yet compliance will be very costly. Thus, because beef producers must spend significant sums to comply or risk significant fines, they will be harmed if review is delayed (VI.D.4.a.ii.). Hence, the case is likely ripe for review, and the court should hear it at this time.

ANALYSIS FOR QUESTION 2

2(a): The issue in Question 2(a) is whether the EPA correctly chose to use notice-and-comment rulemaking rather than formal rulemaking. Turning to III.B.1.a. in the checklist above, you need to analyze whether the EPA was required to use formal rulemaking. Typically, courts apply *Chevron* analysis to determine whether the agency reasonably interpreted its enabling statute (VII.B.4.). At *Chevron*'s step one, a court will look to see whether Congress had directly spoken to this precise issue by examining the enabling statute to see if it includes the phrase "on the record after a hearing" or similar words. If those words are not included, then at *Chevron*'s step two, a court will determine whether the agency's interpretation of the language is reasonable.

Here, Section 2 of the HEAT Act authorized the EPA to issue rules "after opportunity for a full public hearing in which all interested parties may participate." This language is not identical to "on the record after a hearing;" however, the statutory language is not simply "after hearing," which is typically found in statutes, Likely, a court would determine that the included language was not sufficient to trigger formal rulemaking and the EPA's decision to use notice-and-comment rulemaking was reasonable because that process would allow all interested parties to participate. However, be sure to include counter-analysis: that the language suggests Congress intended to allow for more participation than "after hearing" would indicate.

2(b): The issue in Question 2(b) is whether the EPA followed the notice-and-comment rulemaking procedures the APA requires. Turning to III.C.2. in the checklist above, you need to first analyze whether the notice included the time, place, and nature of the public proceedings (if any); the legal authority for the rule; and either the substance of the proposed rule or a description of the subjects and issues involved. Ask: Was the notice sufficient to fairly apprise interested persons of the issues involved so that they may present responsive data or argument? (III.C.2.a.).

In this case, it is likely that the NPRM was "sufficient to fairly apprise interested persons of the issues involved." While the NPRM noted that climate change "is largely caused by human activity" and seemed focused on carbon dioxide emissions, the NPRM mentioned methane gas and the 50 parts per million standard. Moreover, the poultry and pork industries submitted comments, objecting to the extreme effects those requirements would have on their industries. While the beef producers did not believe it was necessary to comment, their failure to comment relates less to their conclusion that the rule would not apply to them and more to their belief the data was so weak that their industry would not be regulated. These facts suggest that the beef producers had sufficient notice.

Returning to the checklist, you should work your way through the next few questions and conclude that no prohibited ex parte occurred (III.C.2.b.), the agency allowed interested parties to submit "written data, views, or arguments" on the proposed rule (III.C.2.c.), and that no hybrid procedures were required (III.C.2.d).

You should note, however, that the final rule differed significantly from the proposed rule (III.C.2.e.). Thus, you will need to determine whether the final rule can be characterized as a "logical outgrowth" of the proposed rule or whether the EPA pulled a "surprise switcheroo." To do so, ask whether the final rule materially altered the issues involved in the rulemaking and whether the final rule substantially departed from the substance of the proposed rule.

In this case, the proposed rule did not target any specific industry, focused on human causes of climate change, targeted companies whose manufacturing or production activities produced carbon dioxide or methane gas, and only discussed the implementation of scrubbers. Airtight buildings and masks were not mentioned, and all industries, rather than one specific industry, were targeted. Hence, it is likely that the final rule was not a logical outgrowth of the proposed rule and the EPA should begin the notice-and-comment rulemaking process again if it wishes to promulgate the final rule.

ANALYSIS FOR QUESTION 3

3(a): The issue in Question 3(a) is whether the EPA's decision would be upheld after judicial review. To answer this question, you need to identify and then apply the appropriate standard of review. To identify the appropriate standard of review, you should turn to VII.A.1. in the checklist above and conclude that the court is reviewing findings of fact made during a notice-and-comment rulemaking; hence, the court will review the agency's finding using the arbitrary and capricious standard (VII.A.1.b).

To apply the arbitrary and capricious standard of review, courts ask the following: was the agency's decision (1) based on a consideration of all the relevant factors, and (2) free of clear error? (Both elements must be satisfied) (VII.B.2.).

You must first identify the factual findings the EPA made in its final rule. Here, the EPA determined that (1) "the primary contributor to climate change is methane gas emissions by cattle, especially in large feedlots;" (2) "methane scrubbers are an efficient method to lower methane gas emissions;" (3) "keeping cattle indoors will also lower emissions;" and (4) "[methane] emissions must be no more than 50 parts per billion for climate change to be reduced." (SOBP). Importantly, EPA offered no evidence to support any of these findings.

Now, to determine whether the agency's decision was based on a consideration of all the relevant factors, check the enabling statute to see what factors, if any, Congress included. The HEAT Act identifies a number of findings in Section 1 and directs the EPA to consider these findings when promulgating regulations. One finding that is inconsistent with the HEAT Act is the EPA's finding that one industry, specifically cattle feedlots, are the primary cause of climate change. Congress, both in the findings section of the HEAT Act and in Act's legislative history, made clear that no one industry should bear the burden of addressing climate change on its own. That appears to have happened here. Hence, the EPA's finding—(1) "the primary contributor to climate change is methane gas emissions by cattle, especially in large feedlots"—is arbitrary and capricious.

Now, to determine whether the agency's decision was free of clear error, look to see if the evidence the agency relied on supports its factual findings. In this case, the EPA did not provide any evidentiary support for its findings; hence, the EPA's findings (2) "methane scrubbers are an efficient method to lower methane gas emissions;" (3) "keeping cattle indoors will also lower emissions;" and (4) "[methane] emissions must be no more than 50 parts per billion for climate change to be reduced" are all arbitrary and capricious.

3(b): The issue in Question 3(b) is whether the EPA's decision would be upheld after judicial review. To answer this question, you need to identify and then apply the appropriate standard of review. To identify the standard of review, you must first identify the language in the statute that the agency interpreted as well as the agency's interpretation. Here, the question tells you that the language in the statute is "any industry that contributes to climate change," and the EPA interpreted that language to apply to one industry: cattle feedlots.

To identify the appropriate standard of review to apply, you should turn to VII.A. in the checklist above and conclude that the court is reviewing a question of law: specifically, the interpretation of language in the HEAT Act, a statute that the EPA administers (VII.A.2.b.iii). Because the EPA made its interpretation during a notice-and-comment rulemaking, the court will review the agency's interpretation using *Chevron* analysis (VII.A.2.b.iii.(a).).

Preliminarily, you should note that a court has not already interpreted the same language differently from the agency, so *Brand X* does not apply (VII.B.4.a.i.). To apply *Chevron*'s two-step analysis (VII.B.4.b), you will first, using the traditional tools of statutory interpretation, determine whether Congress has spoken directly to the precise issue before the court (*Chevron* step one).

Because you represent BPA, you will want to make a strong argument that Congress has directly spoken and the EPA's interpretation conflicts with congressional intent. To do so, start with the text of the statute. Here, you should note that the statute talks about "any industry," not one industry. The dictionary defines "any" to mean "to one or some of a thing or number of things, no matter how much or many." This definition makes clear that the EPA had no authority to target just one industry, as it did. Even if this language were ambiguous, the findings clause specifically states "no one industry should bear the burden of remedying this danger." And even were ambiguity to remain, the bill's sponsor noted during the House floor debates that "No one industry will bear this burden alone." In addition, Congress noted concern with both carbon dioxide and methane, not just methane.

Once you have made BPA's arguments for *Chevron* step one, you need to include the EPA's response as counter-analysis: here, "any industry" can mean just one industry; hence, because the text is unambiguous, there is no need to consider the findings clause or legislative history. In any event, statements made during floor debates and statements from sponsors are not persuasive indicators of congressional intent.

Next, even though you have argued that Congress spoke at *Chevron* step one, you need to finish the *Chevron* analysis. Thus, you would say, assuming the court were to determine that Congress has not directly spoken to the precise issue before the court, the EPA has failed to offer a reasoned explanation for why it chose that interpretation and the interpretation is unreasonable. Here, you note that the EPA failed to explain its changed interpretation. You might also point out that the EPA's regulation will not further the congressional purpose because it targets only one industry and only one congressionally identified cause. Again, include the agency's counter arguments, noting that the interpretation need not be the interpretation the court would prefer, just an interpretation that is within the range of reasonableness.

In sum, a court applying *Chevron* analysis would likely conclude that Congress directly spoke to this issue (step one) and the EPA's interpretation is inconsistent with that congressional intent. Further, even if Congress did not speak clearly and implicitly delegated to the EPA, the EPA failed to offer a reasoned explanation for why it chose an unreasonable interpretation (step two).